D1535531

SPOTLIGHT on MUSIC™

Authors

Judy Bond

René Boyer

Margaret Campbelle-Holman

Emily Crocker

Marilyn C. Davidson

Robert de Frece

Virginia Ebinger

Mary Goetze

Betsy M. Henderson

John Jacobson

Michael Jothen

Chris Judah-Lauder

Carol King

Vincent P. Lawrence

Ellen McCullough-Brabson

Janet McMillion

Nancy L. T. Miller

Ivy Rawlins

Susan Snyder

Gilberto D. Soto

Kodály Contributing Consultant

Sr. Lorna Zemke

ACKNOWLEDGMENTS

From the Top student features are adapted from the nationally distributed public radio program **From the Top:** CEOs/Executive Producers—Jennifer Hurley-Wales, Gerald Slavet; Authors—Ann Gregg, Joanne Robinson

Creative Direction and Delivery: The Quarasan Group, Inc.

From the Top-On National Radio! selections are adapted from the nationally distributed public radio program, *From the Top.* CEOs/Executive Producers: Jennifer Hurley-Wales and Gerald Slavet. Authors: Ann Gregg and Joanne Robinson. © 2000, 2001, 2002, 2003 From the Top, Inc.

Grateful acknowledgment is given to the following authors, composers and publishers. Every effort has been made to trace the ownership of all copyrighted material and to secure the necessary permissions to reprint these selections. In the case of some selections for which acknowledgment is not given, extensive research has failed to locate the copyright holders.

Ame Fure, From Asian-Pacific Islander perceptions of childhood's musical heritage: A collection of children's songs orally transmitted by immigrants and refugees along the Wasatch Front of Utah by Kathy B. Sorensen, Ph.D., University of Utah; pub. by UMI, Copyright 1991 by Kathy B. Sorensen.

America, My Homeland, Words and Music by Robert de Frece and Shirley Funk. Copyright © 1991 by American Orff-Schulwerk Association. International Copyright Secured. All Rights Reserved.

Arroyito serrano (Mountain Stream), Words and Music by Carlos Gustavino. Copyright © 1960 (Renewed) by Ricordi Americana. International Copyright Secured. All Rights Reserved.

At The Hop, Words and Music by Arthur Singer, John Madara and David White. Copyright © 1957 (Renewed) by Arc Music Corporation (BMI) and Six Continents Music Publishing, Inc. (BMI). All Rights Administered by Arc Music Corporation (BMI). International Copyright Secured. All Rights Reserved. Used by Permission.

Bamboo, Words and Music by Dave Van Ronk. Copyright © 1962 (Renewed) PEPAMAR MUSIC CORP. All Rights Administered by WB MUSIC CORP. All Rights Reserved. Used by Permission.

Boogie Woogie Ghost, The, Words and Music by Nadine Pelgar. Copyright © 1973 (Renewed 2001) by Scholastic, Inc. International Copyright Secured. All Rights Reserved.

Circle of Song, Words and Music by Emily Crocker. Copyright © 2000 by HAL LEONARD CORPORATION. International Copyright Secured. All Rights Reserved.

December Nights, December Lights, Words and Music by Emily Crocker. Copyright © 2000 by MUSIC EXPRESS, LLC. International Copyright Secured. All Rights Reserved.

Don't Let the Music Stop, Words Adapted from Walt Whitman and Arthur O'Shaughnessy. Additional Words and Music by Eugene Butler. Copyright © 1978 by Heritage Music Press. International Copyright Secured. All Rights Reserved.

Down at the Twist and Shout, Words and Music by Mary Chapin Carpenter © 1990 EMI APRIL MUSIC INC. and GETAREALJOB MUSIC. All Rights Controlled and Administered by EMI APRIL MUSIC INC. All Rights Reserved. International Copyright Secured. Used by Permission.

E nănă kăkou i nă manu, (Look at the Birds in the Sky), Words and Music by Herbert Mahelona and Stacey Naki. Copyright © 1999 by Plymouth Music Co., Inc. International Copyright Secured. All Rights Reserved.

Follow Your Dream, Words and Music by Mary Donnelly. Copyright © 1990 by Alfred Publishing Co., Inc. International Copyright Secured. All Rights Reserved.

Grandma's Feather Bed, Words and Music by Jim Connor. Copyright © 1973; Renewed 2001 Cherry River Music Co. (BMI) and Songs of DreamWorks (BMI). Worldwide Rights for Songs Of DreamWorks Administered by Cherry River Music Co. International Copyright Secured. All Rights Reserved.

Happiness from YOU'RE A GOOD MAN, CHARLIE BROWN. Words and Music by Clark Gesner. © 1965 JEREMY MUSIC INC. © Renewed 1993 MPL MUSIC PUBLISHING, INC. All Rights on behalf of NOTABLE MUSIC CO., INC. Administered by WB MUSIC CORP. Print Rights on behalf of EMI CARWIN CATALOG INC. Administered by WARNER BROS. PUBLICATIONS U.S. INC. All Rights Reserved.

Happy Talk from SOUTH PACIFIC. Words by Oscar Hammerstein II. Music by Richard Rodgers. Copyright © 1949 by Williamson Music. All Rights Reserved.

Hey, Look Me Over from WILD CAT. Words by Carolyn Leigh. Music by Cy Coleman. Copyright © 1960 Carolyn Leigh and Cy Coleman. All Rights Throughout the World Controlled by EDWIN H. MORRIS & COMPANY, A Division of MPL Communications, Inc. All Rights Reserved.

Hine Ma Tov (How Good It Is). Words from Psalm 133:1. Music by Allen E. Naplan. © by Boosey & Hawkes, Inc. International Copyright Secured. All Rights Reserved. Used by Permission.

I Heard a Mockingbird, Words and Music by Carol King and Rebecca Treadway. Copyright © by Carol King and Rebecca Treadway. International Copyright Secured. All Rights Reserved.

I'll Rise When the Rooster Crows, Appalachian Folk Song. Music by Uncle Dave Macon. Copyright © 1983 Butterside Music. International Copyright Secured. All Rights Reserved.

It's the Hard-Knock Life, From MTI's Broadway Junior Broadway for Kids ANNIE Junior. Music by Charles Strouse. Lyrics by Martin Charnin. Music and Lyrics Copyright © 1977, 1978 by Edwin H. Morris & Co, a Division of MPL Communications, Inc. and Charles Strouse. All Rights Reserved. Used by Permission.

I Think I'm Gonna Like It Here, From MTI's Broadway Junior Broadway for Kids ANNIE Junior. Music by Charles Strouse. Lyrics by Martin Charnin. Music and Lyrics Copyright © 1977, 1978 by Edwin H. Morris & Co, a Division of MPL Communications, Inc. and Charles Strouse. All Rights Reserved. Used by Permission.

I Will Be Your Friend, Words and Music by Guy Davis. Copyright © 2003 by Southern Poverty Law Center. International Copyright Secured. All Rights Reserved.

Just One Planet, Words and Music by Sarah Stevens and Catherine Marchese. Copyright © by One Planet, Inc. International Copyright Secured. All Rights Reserved.

La otra España (The Other Spain), Words and Music by Juan C. Calderon. Copyright © by ED. MUSICALES POLYGRAM S.A./DISCORA-MA. All rights administered in the United States and Canada by UNIVERSAL - POLYGRAM INTERNATIONAL PUBLISHING, INC. International Copyright Secured. All Rights Reserved.

Loco-Motion, The, Words and Music by Gerry Goffin and Carole King. © 1962 (Renewed 1990) SCREEN GEMS-EMI MUSIC INC. International Copyright Secured. All Rights Reserved. Used by Permission.

Modern Dragon, A, by Rowena Bastin Bennett, from *Songs Around a Toadstool Table,* Copyright 1930, 1937, 1965 by Follett Publishing Company. Reprinted in *Piping Down the Valleys Wild,* edited by Nancy Larrick. Published by Delacorte Press, Copyright © 1968, 1985. All rights reserved.

Mighty River, by Will Brecht. Used by Permission.

Morning Has Broken, Words by Eleanor Farjeon. Music Traditional Gaelic Melody. Words Copyright © 1957 by Eleanor Farjeon c/o David Higham & Associates. International Copyright Secured. All Rights Reserved.

My Town, My World, Words and Music by John Jacobson and John Higgins. Copyright © 2003 by HAL LEONARD CORPORATION. International Copyright Secured. All Rights Reserved.

continued on page 409

The **McGraw-Hill** Companies

 **Macmillan McGraw-Hill**

Published by Macmillan/McGraw-Hill, of McGraw-Hill Education, a division of The McGraw-Hill Companies, Inc., Two Penn Plaza, New York, New York 10121.

Copyright © 2005 by Macmillan/McGraw-Hill. All rights reserved. No part of this publication may be reproduced or distributed in any form or by any means, or stored in a database or retrieval system, without the prior written consent of The McGraw-Hill Companies, Inc., including, but not limited to, network storage or transmission, or broadcast for distance learning.

Printed in the United States of America
ISBN 0-02-295677-8 / 4
3 4 5 6 7 8 9 058/043 10 09 08 07 06 05 04

CONTRIBUTORS

Consultants

Brian Burnett,
Movement

Stephen Gabriel,
Technology

Magali Iglesias,
English Language Learners

Roberta Newcomer,
Special Learners/Assessment

Frank Rodríguez,
English Language Learners

Jacque Schrader,
Movement

Kathy B. Sorensen,
International Phonetic
Alphabet

Patti Windes-Bridges,
Listening Maps

Linda Worsley,
Listening/Singable
English Translations

Sr. Lorna Zemke,
Kodály Contributing
Consultant

Contributing Writers

Allison Abucewicz
Sharon Berndt
Rhona Brink
Ann Burbridge
Debbie Helm Daniel
Katherine Domingo
Kari Gilbertson
Janet Graham
Hilree Hamilton
Linda Harley
Judy Henneberger
Carol Huffman
Bernie Hynson, Jr.
Sheila A. Kerley
Ellen Mendelsohn

Cristi Cary Miller
Leigh Ann Mock
Patricia O'Rourke
Barbara Resch
Isabel Romero
Carl B. Schmidt
Debra Shearer
Ellen Mundy Shuler
Carol Wheeler
Sheila Woodward

Recordings

Executive Producer
John Higgins

Senior Music Editor/Producer
Emily Crocker

Senior Recording Producer
Mark Brymer

Recording Producers
Steve Millikan
Andy Waterman

Associate Recording Producers
Alan Billingsley, Darrell
Bledsoe, Stacy Carson,
Emily Crocker, Rosanna

Eckert, John Egan,
Chad Evans, Darlene
Koldenhoven,
Chris Koszuta, Don
Markese, Matthew
McGregor, Steve Potts,
Edwin Schupman, Michael
Spresser, Frank Stegall,
David Vartanian, Mike
Wilson, Ted Wilson

Project/Mastering Engineer
Mark Aspinall

Post Production Engineer
Don Sternecker

Multicultural Consultants

William Anderson, Chet-Yeng Loong, Edwin Schupman, Kathy B. Sorensen, Gilberto D. Soto, Judith Cook Tucker, Dennis Waring

In the Spotlight Consultant

Willa Dunlevy

Multicultural Advisors

Brad Ahawanrathe Bonaparte (Mohawk), Emmanuel Akakpo (Ewe), Earlene Albano (Hawaiian), Luana Au (Maori), Ruby Beeston (Mandarin), Latif Bolat (Turkey), Estella Christensen (Spanish), Oussama Davis (Arabic), Mia Delguardo (Minahasa), Nolutho Ndengane Diko (Xhosa), Angela Fields (Hopi, Chemehuevi), Gary Fields (Lakota, Cree), Gilad Harel (Hebrew), Josephine Hetarihon (Bahasa Indonesian, Minahasa, and Maluko dialect), Judy Hirt-Manheimer (Hebrew), Rose Jakub (Navajo), Elizabeth Jarema (Fijian), Rita Jensen (Swedish), Malou Jewett (Visayan), Alejandro Jimenez (Hispanic), Chris Jones (Hungarian), Wendy Jyang Shamo (Mandarin), Amir Kalay (Hebrew), Michael Katsan (Greek), Silvi Madarajan (Tamil), Georgia Magpie (Comanche), Nona Mardi (Malay), Aida Mattingly (Tagalog), Mike Kanathohare McDonald (Mohawk), Vasana de Mel (Sinhala), Marion Miller (Czech), Etsuko Miskin (Japanese), Mogens Mogenson (Danish), Kenny Tahawisoren Perkins (Mohawk), Pradeep Nayyar (Punjabi, Hindi), Renu Nayyar (Punjabi), Mfanego Ngwenya (Zulu), Wil Numkena (Hopi), Samuel Owuru (Akan), Nina Padukone (Konkani), Hung Yong Park (Korean), James Parker (Finnish), Jose Pereira (Konkani), Berrit Price (Norwegian), John Rainer (Taos Pueblo, Creek), Lillian Rainer (Taos Pueblo, Creek, Apache), Arnold Richardson (Haliwa-Saponi), Ken Runnacles (German), Trudy Shenk (German), Ron Singer (Navajo), Ernest Sive (Cahuilla, Serrano [Maringa']), Bonnie Slade (Swedish), Cristina Sorrentino (Portuguese), Diane Thram (Xhosa), Elena Todorov (Bulgarian), Zlatina Todorov (Russian), Tom Toronto (Lao, Thai), Rebecca Wilberg (French, Italian), Sheila Woodward (Zulu), Keith Yackeyonny (Comanche)

Contents

Spotlight on Music Reading.........241

Spotlight on Performance............289

Spotlight on Celebrations............353

In the Spotlight

Let's sing the songs of America!
Let's play the tunes of people and places,
old and new, grand and small.
Let's sing the songs of the cities and states,
the beach and the prairie,
the skies and the seas.
Beat the drum! Sound the trumpet!
Step into the light!
Let's sing the songs of America!

Step into the Spotlight

Spotlight CD
Track 1

Words and Music by John Jacobson,
Emily Crocker, and John Higgins

1. Lis - ten to the world a - round you, There is
2. In a world of sound and col - or, in a

mus - ic ev - 'ry - where.___ Just step out - side___ your
rhy - thm all it's own,___ It's the heart - beat of___ A -

door - way, and you can hear mus - ic in the air!___
mer - i - ca, the land we proud - ly call our home!_

From the cit - y to the farm and field,___ to the
From the cit - y to the farm and field,___ there's a

A

The songs of America are rich and varied.
They remind us of where we are,
where we have been,
where we are going,
and sometimes
where we long to be.

SHENANDOAH

Spotlight CD
Track 4

Traditional Sea Chanty

A7 D   G D

1. Oh, Shen - an - doah,___ I long to hear you.
2. Oh, Shen - an - doah,___ I'm bound to leave you.
3. 'Tis sev'n long years___ since last I saw you.

G   D

A - way,_____ you roll - ing riv - er.
A - way,_____ you roll - ing riv - er.
A - way,_____ you roll - ing riv - er.

Bm   D G

Oh, Shen - an - doah,___ I long to hear you.
Oh, Shen - an - doah,___ I'll not de - ceive you.
'Tis sev'n long years___ since last I saw you.

A D   F#m G

A - way,_____ I'm bound a - way
A - way,_____ I'm bound a - way
A - way,_____ I'm bound a - way

Em7   A7   D D

'cross the wide Mis - sour - i.
'cross the wide Mis - sour - i.
'cross the wide Mis - sour - i.

D

The songs of America remind us of our favorite places, whether "On Top of Old Smokey," "Down by the Riverside," or having lots of fun at Grandma's house!

Grandma's FEATHER BED

Spotlight CD
Track 7

Words and Music by Jim Conner

Verse

When I was a lit-tle-bit-ty boy
Af-ter sup-per we'd sit a-round the fire, the

just up off-a-the floor,
old folks-'d spit and chew,

We used to go down to
Pa would talk a-bout the

Grand-ma's house ev-'ry month end or so,
farm and the war and Gramy'd sing a bal-lad or two.

We'd have
I'd

chick-en pie and coun-try ham and
sit and lis-ten and watch the fire till the

home-made but-ter on the bread,
cob-webs filled my head,

But the best thing of all a-bout
Next thing I'd know I'd

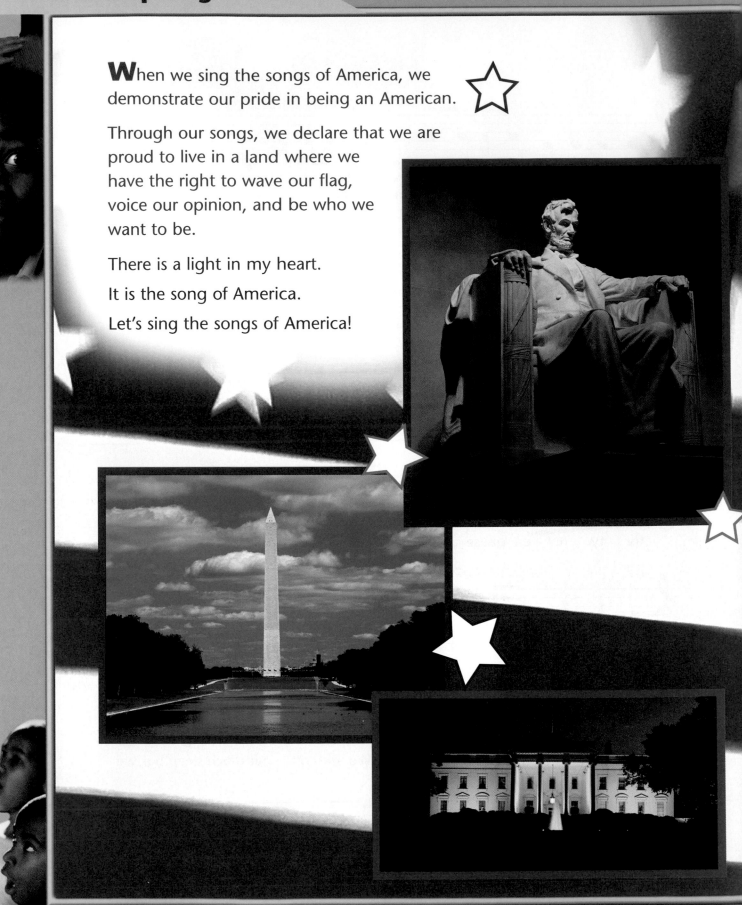

When we sing the songs of America, we demonstrate our pride in being an American.

Through our songs, we declare that we are proud to live in a land where we have the right to wave our flag, voice our opinion, and be who we want to be.

There is a light in my heart.

It is the song of America.

Let's sing the songs of America!

Patriotic Medley

 **Spotlight CD
Track 10**

Words by George M. Cohan,
Woody Guthrie, and Katharine Lee Bates.

You're a Grand Old Flag

You're a Grand Old Flag, you're a high flyin' flag.
And forever in peace may you wave.
You're the emblem of the land I love,
The home of the free and the brave.
Ev'ry heart beats true
   for the red, white, and blue,
Where there's never a boast or brag.
But should auld acquaintance be forgot,
Keep your eye on the grand old flag.

This Land Is Your Land

This land is your land, this land is my land
From California to the New York Island.
From the redwood forest
   to the Gulf Stream waters,
This land was made for you and me.
As I was walking that ribbon of highway,
I saw above me that endless skyway.
I saw below me that golden valley.
This land was made for you and me.

America!

America! America! God shed His grace on thee.
And crown thy good with brotherhood,
From sea to shining sea!

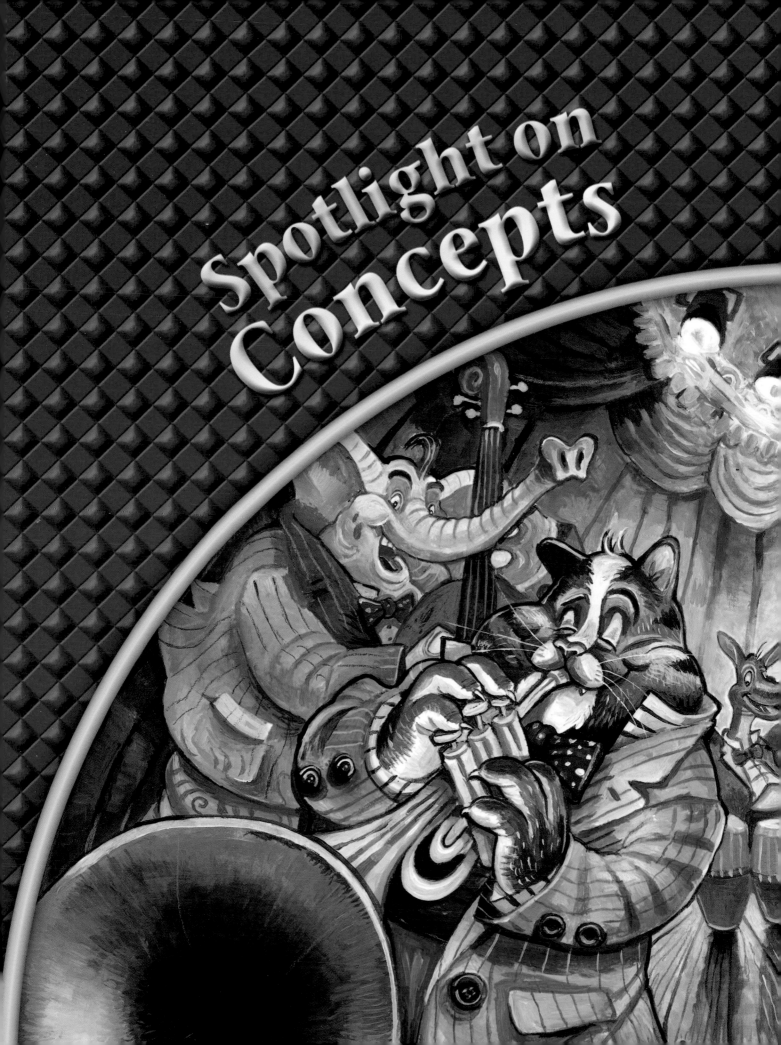

Spotlight on
Concepts

Spotlight on Concepts

Spotlight on Concepts

UNIT 1

Music for Everyone

Music is for everyone. No matter who you are, where you are from, or what you like, music has something for you! In Unit 1 you will sing, play, listen, and create music that you can enjoy and share with others.

Coming Attractions

Move to a folk song from Spain.

Listen to and sing a Native American lullaby.

Sing a fun rock and roll song.

Music can express messages of happiness, hope, and friendship. "Something for Me, Something for You" is a song about how a little sharing between friends can make a big difference. What can you do to make a difference in someone's life?

Something for ME, Something for YOU

CD 1:1

Words and Music by J.D. Steele, Larry Long, Brian C. Herron and Nate Underwood

Refrain

Some-thing for me,____ some-thing for you,____ you show love for me,____ I show love for you.____ If we take time to see____ what this world could be____ we could live peace-ful - ly,____ we all could be free.

Verse (Rap)

1. I'm the voice of the future
The next in charge
So this world's up to us to
Protect from harm
It's about love and peace and
Respecting each other
You shouldn't judge somebody
Just because of their color
Yo!
We're all a little different
Something unique
But these same differences
Make the world complete
Whether boy or girl –
Put-downs is wack!
We need to show each other
   support
Instead of all that
Fightin' just ain't the answer
We need to talk
And get past all the hate
So we can see it resolved
And, adults, understand that
We learn from you
Everything in this world that
A person should do
Peace works for everybody
Meaning me and you
And we can make Dr. King's
Dream really come true
Take time, spread love
And believe in you
And together we can learn to
Put love to use

Refrain

2. Sometimes I get sad at what
I hear on the news
Or when I see kids getting
Into fights at school
I know all are equal
That means we're all one
Not saying there aren't
   differences
That we need to love
We gotta learn patience
And know what's right
We might disagree
But we don't have to fight
Respect is respect and we
Need to show it
That's why we came together
On this song
So you could know it
Since we're the future
We're telling you now
All the racism and hatred
We're shutting it down
We live and we learn
And we share with one another
And smile at the new things
That we discover
And it's all from the heart
Meaning nothing but love
And we're gonna make better
What was given to us
It don't matter if you're out
   of town
Or live on my street
Just try to be a friend to
Whoever you meet
And make peace!

Refrain

Taking the Pulse of Music

CONCEPT
METER

SKILLS
SING, LISTEN, DESCRIBE

LINKS
FINE ART, MOVEMENT

When you put a finger on your wrist, you can feel the steady beat of your pulse. Music also has a steady pulse. It is called **beat**. Beats in music are felt in groups of strong and weak beats.

Listen for the strong and weak beats in "My Town, My World."
Sing the song.

MY TOWN, MY WORLD

CD 1:4

Words and Music by
John Jacobson and John Higgins

I'm on - ly one per-son, an in-di-vid - u-al.

You've got your own life, too.— The feel-ing's nat-u-ral, But

our lives are con-nect - ed with ev-'ry boy and girl.— We're a

fam-i-ly, a neigh-bor-hood, a coun-try and a world.—

My town,— my world!— My town,— my world!—

My street and my neigh-bor-hood, I know each mile holds some-thing good! My town, my world! My town, my world!

Heart to heart and face to face, each a part of the hu-man race, tak-ing care of our spe-cial place, my town, my

world! Yes, world! My town, my world!

Group the Beat

Which pattern below shows the beat groupings for "My Town, My World"?

Meter signatures, such as $\frac{2}{4}$, $\frac{3}{4}$, and $\frac{4}{4}$ are found at the beginning of songs. The top number shows the number of beats in each group or measure. The bottom number shows which note gets the beat.

Identify the meter signature in "My Town, My World."

$\frac{2}{4}$ can also be written like this: $\frac{2}{4}$

$\frac{4}{4}$ can also be written like this: $\frac{4}{4}$

Art Gallery

Child with a Dove
Pablo Picasso (1881–1973) created this drawing in 1901. The dove is a symbol for peace.

THINK!

Read the words of "My Town, My World." What do Picasso's painting and this song have in common?

Listen to "Hush, Little Baby."

Bobby McFerrin and Yo-Yo Ma ▶

LISTENING CD 1:7

Hush, Little Baby American folk song

The song has three verses and is a **duet** performed by Yo–Yo Ma and Bobby McFerrin. In a duet, two musicians play or sing together. **Describe** how McFerrin uses his voice when he is not singing words.

Practice the movements below.

PAT (1 beat)

CROSS (1 beat)

CLAP (1 beat)

THUMBS UP (2 beats)

Perform the movements in this order each time you hear the duet in "Hush, Little Baby." **Move** to the beat.

1	PAT	PAT	CROSS	CROSS
2	PAT	PAT	CROSS	CROSS
3	PAT	CLAP	PAT	CLAP
4	THUMBS UP		THUMBS UP	

Shape Up and Ship Out!

CONCEPT
MELODY
SKILLS
SING, DESCRIBE, COMPARE
LINKS
SOCIAL STUDIES, CULTURES

Just as waves in the ocean rise and fall, the **pitch** of "Somos el barco" also goes up and down. Pitch is the highness and lowness of a sound.

Sing the song.

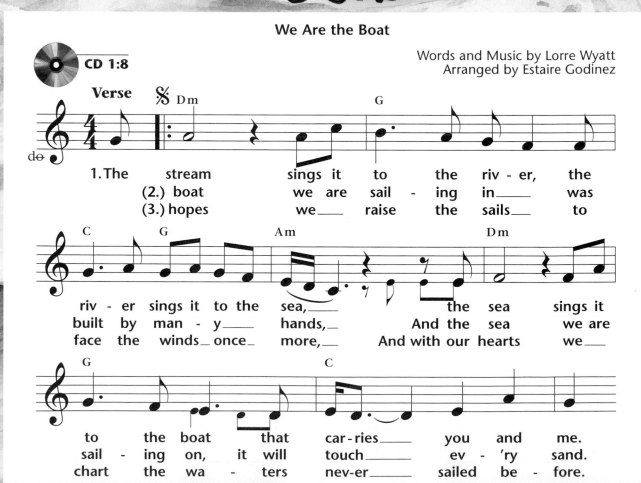

We Are the Boat

CD 1:8

Words and Music by Lorre Wyatt
Arranged by Estaire Godinez

1. The stream sings it to the riv - er, the
(2.) boat we are sail - ing in____ was
(3.) hopes we____ raise the sails____ to

riv - er sings it to the sea,____ the sea sings it
built by man - y____ hands,____ And the sea we are
face the winds__ once__ more,____ And with our hearts we____

to the boat that car - ries____ you and me.
sail - ing on, it will touch____ ev - 'ry sand.
chart the wa - ters nev-er____ sailed be - fore.

Move your hand up and down with the shape of the **melody**.
A melody is a series of pitches that moves upward, downward,
or stays the same.

The Contour Connection

Imagine you are hiking along a mountain trail. You will go up and down many times. In music, the ups and downs of a melody are known as **contour**.

"A la puerta del cielo" is a folk song from Spain.

Sing the song. **Identify** where the melody moves up and where the melody moves down.

MAP
FRANCE
PORTUGAL
SPAIN
MOROCCO   ALGERIA

A la puerta del cielo
At the Gate of Heaven

CD 1:12

Spanish Folk Song
English Version by MMH

Spanish: A la puer-ta del cie-lo ven-den za-pa-tos,
Pronunciation: a la pwer ta ðel sye lo βen den sa pa tos
English: At the gate of Heav'n they are sell-ing *za-pa-tos*,

Pa-ra los an-ge-li-tos que an-dan des-cal-zos.
pa ra los ang xe li tos kean dan des kai sos
For the lit-tle an-gels who go walk-ing bare-foot.

Duér-me-te, ni-ño, duér-me-te, ni-ño,
dwer me te ni nyo dwer me te ni nyo
Slum-ber my ba-by, slum-ber my ba-by,

Duér-me-te, ni-ño, a-rru, a-rru.
dwer me te ni nyo a r̄u a r̄u
slum-ber my ba-by, a-rru, a-rru.

Compare these contour lines with each line of the song. Which contour line appears twice in the song?

 LISTENING CD 1:16

English horn

Adagio from *Concierto de Aranjuez* (excerpt) by Joaquín Rodrigo

This recording features guitar and English horn with orchestra.

Listen for the English horn playing the melody in "Adagio" from *Concierto de Aranjuez*. Trace the contour of the melody in the air with your hand as you listen again.

Meet the Musician

Joaquín Rodrigo (1901–1999), composer, was born in Valencia, Spain. At age three he was blinded by an illness, yet he still learned to play the piano and violin. He wrote over sixty songs and many choral and instrumental works. Rodrigo said his blindness led him to music. "I remember the song of the crickets, the pounding of the waves, the sound of the organ, and the church bells in my hometown."

CD-ROM

Use *Orchestral Instruments* **CD-ROM** to learn more about the English horn and other instruments of the orchestra.

LESSON 3

CONCEPT
RHYTHM
SKILLS
READ, PLAY, SING
LINKS
LANGUAGE ARTS, SOCIAL STUDIES

Rhythm, Round, Fun!

This speech piece is about traveling the globe. If you could go anywhere on the planet, where would you go?

Read "A Journey."

CD 1:17

A JOURNEY

Let's go on a jour-ney. Where shall we go?

Pick some plac-es on the plan-et. There's so much to know.

Tra-vel to the con-tin-ents. There's so much to see.

Get your lug-gage load-ed up. Come with me!

All music has sounds and silences of different lengths. These sounds and silences, organized around beat, make up the **rhythm** of a piece. Look at the rhythm symbols below.

♩	**quarter note**	one sound to a beat
♫	two **eighth notes**	two sounds to a beat
♪	**half note**	sound lasting two beats
𝄽	**quarter rest**	silence the length of a beat

Identify some of these rhythms in "A Journey."

Play these rhythm patterns on percussion instruments as you perform "A Journey" again.

Playalong

THINK! **Compare** these two rhythm patterns. If you substitute the first pattern for the first measure of "A Journey," would it work? Why or why not?

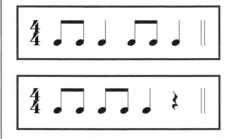

Canon and Round

When two or more voices perform the same melody but start at different times it is called a **round**. Singing a round is fun! The music can go on as long as the singers wish.

Sing the melody of "Peace Round." Then sing it as a round with the class.

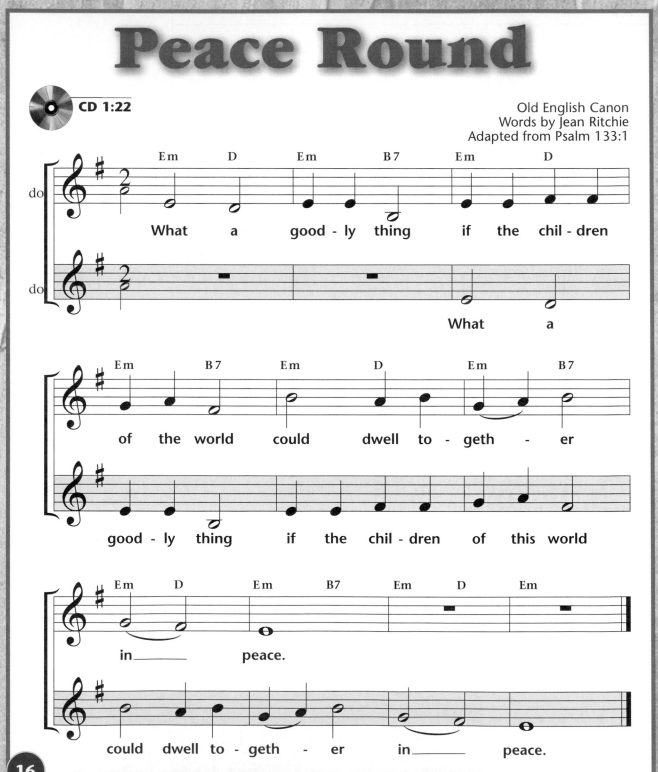

Peace Round

CD 1:22

Old English Canon
Words by Jean Ritchie
Adapted from Psalm 133:1

do | Em D Em B7 Em D
What a good - ly thing if the chil - dren

do | What a

Em B7 Em D Em B7
of the world could dwell to - geth - er

good - ly thing if the chil - dren of this world

Em D Em B7 Em D Em
in_____ peace.

could dwell to - geth - er in_____ peace.

16

A round is a type of **canon**. Canon can have a melody performed in different ways at the same time.

Listen to *Canon in D*. **Compare** it to "Peace Round."

 LISTENING CD 1:26

Canon in D by Johann Pachelbel

Canon in D was written almost three hundred years ago for string instruments. This recording features percussion instruments.

Meet the Musician

Brian Slawson (b. 1957) plays percussion for many different styles of music. He has played with such musicians as blues guitarist Stevie Ray Vaughan and the conductor and composer Leonard Bernstein. Brian studied at The Juilliard School of Music in New York City. He paid for his school by playing marimba on the streets of the city!

Read these rhythm patterns using body percussion.

Perform each pattern above four times as you listen to *Canon in D* again. Then start with pattern 8 and go backwards, reading each pattern four times.

Melodies Take Shape

CONCEPT
MELODY
SKILLS
SING, LISTEN, DESCRIBE
LINKS
FINE ART, CULTURES

Almost everywhere in the world, people have quiet songs they sing to comfort babies and put them to sleep. These songs are called **lullabies**. "Bu-Vah" is a lullaby of the Hopi, a Native American tribe in Arizona.

Sing the song. Trace the melody with your finger as you sing.

BU-VAH

Sleep

CD 1:27

Hopi Lullaby
As sung by Tsung–ayah

Hopi: Bu - u Va - ah_____ ah Bu va-ah Ba va-ah_____
Pronunciation: bu va a bu va bu va

su bü ba veh - e - e_____ eh Bu va-ah Bu va-ah_____
su bü ba vɛ e ɛ bu va bu va

Ko - kyang oh yaht u - u_____ u Bu va-ah Bu va-ah_____
ko kyang ho yat ʋ ʋ bu va bu va

nah i kwe o Kyang u - u - u Bu va-ah Bu va-ah_____
na i kwe o kyang ʋ ʋ bu va bu va

Bu va-ah Bu va-ah_____ Bu va-ah
bu va bu va bu va

Listen to an original recording of "Bu-Vah."

  **CD 1:29**

Bu-Vah Hopi Lullaby

This recording features "Bu-Vah" sung by Tsung–ayah, a Hopi singer.

THINK!   **Describe** how "Bu-Vah" is like other lullabies that you know.

Learn About Hopi Culture

The Hopi are a unique Native American tribe living in the northeast of Arizona. They trace their roots in North America all the way back to A.D. 500. The Hopi people created many unique methods of farming to adapt to the dry climate of the southwestern region of North America. Farming is a way of life for the Hopi. A Hopi farmer once said, "This is not about growing vegetables; it is about growing kids."

 Art Gallery

This plaque with traditional Hopi designs was made of wicker by Hopi women in Arizona.

Shape That Melody

The shape, or contour, of a melody is formed when pitches move up, down, or repeat.

"Li'l 'Liza Jane" is a folk song from the eastern United States. **Sing** the song.

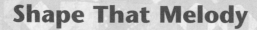

CD 2:1

American Dance-Game Song

1. There's a gal in Bal - ti - more, Li'l 'Li - za Jane,
2. Come, my love, and mar - ry me, Li'l 'Li - za Jane,
3. If you'll come and be my own, Li'l 'Li - za Jane,
4. We'll have chick - ens 'round our door, Li'l 'Li - za Jane,

She's the one that I a - dore, Li'l 'Li - za Jane.
I will take good care of thee, Li'l 'Li - za Jane.
We'll eat ham and sweet corn pone, Li'l 'Li - za Jane.
Brus - sels car - pet on our floor, Li'l 'Li - za Jane.

Refrain

O E - li - za, Li'l 'Li - za Jane,

O E - li - za, Li'l 'Li - za Jane.

The first and third time you sing the words "Li'l 'Liza Jane," the melody is shaped liked this.

Li'l

'Li-

Jane

za

The second and fourth times you sing those words, the melody is shaped like this.

Li'l   'Li-

za

Jane

MIDI

Use "Li'l 'Liza Jane" from **Spotlight on MIDI** for more practice with identifying the contour of a melody.

The melody for the verse of "Li'l 'Liza Jane" uses five different pitches: **do re mi so la** . This set of five pitches is called a **pentatonic scale**.

do   do   re   mi   so   la

Name the pitch syllables in each pattern below. Use the pentatonic scale above as a guide.

do

do

The **tonal center** of a song is the home tone, or the pitch around which the melody is centered. The tonal center of "Li'l 'Liza Jane" is *do*. **Identify** *do* each time it occurs in "Li'l 'Liza Jane."

CONCEPT
FORM

SKILLS
SING, ANALYZE, LISTEN

LINKS
SOCIAL STUDIES, CULTURES

A paragraph is made up of sentences. Music has sentences, too. A musical sentence is called a **phrase**. A phrase is a short section of a song, or other piece of music, that is a complete musical thought.

The melody of "Morning Has Broken" is Gaelic, originally from the Isle of Man in the British Isles.

Sing "Morning Has Broken."
Identify each phrase of the song.

Morning Has Broken

CD 2:4

Traditional Gaelic Melody
Words by Eleanor Farjeon

1. Morn-ing has bro - ken   Like the first morn - ing,
2. Sweet the rain's new   fall   Sun - lit from heav - en,

Black-bird has spo - ken   Like the first   bird.____
Like the first dew - fall   On the first   grass.____

Praise for the sing - ing!   Praise for the morn - ing!
Praise for the sweet - ness   Of the wet gar - den,

Praise for them, spring - ing   Fresh from the   world!____
Sprung in com - plete - ness   Where His feet   pass.____

Listen to another recording of "Morning Has Broken."

 LISTENING CD 2:7

Morning Has Broken traditional Gaelic melody

This recording of "Morning Has Broken" features the singer Cat Stevens.

Listen closely for all of the instruments in the recording.

synthesizer

Meet the Musician

Cat Stevens (b. 1948), singer, was born Steven Demetre Georgiou in London, England. When he picked up a guitar and started writing songs, he changed his name to Cat Stevens. He toured the world and sold over 25 million albums. In 1979 Stevens became a Muslim and changed his name to Yusuf Islam. He left public life and started an Islamic school. He has since dedicated his life to serving the British Muslim community.

guitar

piano

Global Voices

Phrases from South Africa

"Vinqo" is a song of the Zulu people, who live in South Africa. The Zulu and Xhosa people live in the same part of South Africa.

 LISTENING CD 2:8

Vinqo Zulu Song from South Africa

The singers of "Vinqo" are Xhosa children. The words of the song are nonsense, but fun for the children to sing. Listen for the tongue clicks when the children are singing. This is part of the way they pronounce words in their language.

Listen to "Vinqo." **Move** to it as you listen again.

Zulu woman performing a traditional dance

The Zulu people are known for their beautiful beadwork. They send each other messages with these beads.

A Xhosa dancer in South Africa

Follow the translation of "Vinqo" below as you listen to the song again.

MAP
BOTSWANA
NAMIBIA
LESOTHO
SOUTH AFRICA

Vinqo

VERSE

Uph' unyoko? Vinqo!

Usal' ekhaya. Vinqo!

Usaleleni? Vinqo!

Ulunyw' imbengolo. Vinqo!

Imlume kuphi? Vinqo!

Emlenzeni Vinqo!

REFRAIN (sung twice)
Sawubona khanda lentulo

Ngomcwabosi ngomphothulo nkomo

Zobuy' emasisweni. Vinqo!

VERSE

Where is Granny?

She stayed home.

Why did she stay home?

She was bitten by a donkey.

Where was she bitten?

On her leg.

REFRAIN (sung twice)
Hello, head of the lizard!

Pound the maize into flour.

The cattle will be returned from where they were lent.

What's the Form?

Just like sentences make up a paragraph, phrases make up **form** in music. The structure, or plan, of a piece of music is called form.

Use lowercase letters to outline the form of the phrases in music. The first phrase is **a**.
The next phrase will be **a** if it is the same, **b** if it is different.
The musical outline of "Vinqo" is **a a a a a a b b**.

Listen to "Vinqo" again, following the form.

The Music of Running Water

CONCEPT
TONE COLOR

SKILLS
SING, PLAY, READ

LINKS
SOCIAL STUDIES,
LANGUAGE ARTS

"**A**me fure" is a song from Japan that describes the sound of rain. **Sing** the song.

MAP
RUSSIA
CHINA
NORTH KOREA
JAPAN
SOUTH KOREA

Ame fure
Rain

CD 2:9

Collected and Transcribed by
Kathy B. Sorensen
English Words by Linda Worsley

Japanese: あ め あ め ふ れ ふ れ かあ さ ん ガ
Pronunciation: a me a me fu ɾe fu ɾe ka sa ŋ ga
English: **Rain - ing, rain - ing, Now the rain is fall - ing all a - round.**

じゃ の め で お む か え う れ しい な
ja no me de o mu ka e u ɾe shi na
Rain on my um - brel - la makes a ver - y gen - tle sound.

ぴ ち ぴ ち ちゃ ぷ ちゃ ぷ らん らん らん
pi chi pi chi cha pu cha pu ɾan ɾan ɾan
Pi - chi, pi - chi, cha - pu, cha - pu, Hear the rain.

CD-ROM

Use *World Instruments* **CD-ROM** to learn about musical instruments from Japan.

26

Play these rhythm patterns on percussion instruments as you sing "Ame fure."

Read this haiku about rain. Haiku is a form of poetry originally from Japan that has exactly seventeen syllables.

Rain

Rain drenches pale leaves
dark wood railing, road beyond.
I feel like singing.

—*M.A. Mohanraj*

THINK! What kind of body percussion could you perform that would sound like rain? **Perform** your body percussion while a partner reads the haiku above.

Listening for Water

Water has many different sounds. You hear it when rain falls. You hear it as a stream rushes by. You even hear it as it drops over a waterfall.

 LISTENING CD 2:13

Miniwanka (or The Moments of Water) (excerpt)
by R. Murray Schafer

The Canadian composer R. Murray Schafer (b. 1933) wrote "Miniwanka (or The Moments of Water)" to capture the sounds of water. He used different words for water from the languages of the Native American peoples of the American Northwest and Western Canada. In addition to "Miniwanka," he has written many works for orchestra, chorus, and musical theater, as well as multimedia pieces on computer. Besides being a composer, Schafer is also known as an educator, environmentalist, literary scholar, and a visual artist.

Listen to "Miniwanka" for how the singers change the **tone color** of their voices to create the sound of a rain shower. Tone color is the term used to describe the sound of an instrument or voice.

Follow the listening map below as you listen to "Miniwanka" again.

**Listening Map for Miniwanka
(or The Moments of Water) (excerpt)**

Melodies with Shape

CONCEPT
MELODY
SKILLS
SING, DESCRIBE, PLAY
LINKS
DANCE

"**O**ctopus's Garden" is a fun song to sing.

Sing "Octopus's Garden." How might you move to show the beat and shape of the melody?

Octopus's Garden

CD 2:14

Words and Music by Richard Starkey

1. I'd   like   to   be____   un - der   the   sea____
He'd   let   us   in____   knows   where   we've   been____

____   in an Oct - o - pus - 's Gar   -   den   in   the   shade.
____   in his Oct - o - pus - 's Gar   -   den   in   the   shade.

1. I'd   ask   my   friends   to   come   and   see____

an   Oct - o - pus - 's   Gar - den with   me.____

I'd like to be____   un-der the sea____   in an

2. We would be warm below the storm
in our little hideaway beneath the waves.
Resting our head on the seabed
in an Octopus's Garden near a cave.
We would sing and dance around
because we know we can't be found.

Fun with a Canon

"Old Abram Brown" is from a song collection called *Friday Afternoons*. This collection was written for students to have fun songs to sing on a Friday afternoon.

Sing the song. Then sing it again as a canon.

Old Abram Brown

CD 2:17

Music by Benjamin Britten
Words by Walter de la Mare

1 Old A - bram Brown is dead and gone,

2 You'll nev - er see him more.

3 He used to wear a long brown coat

4 That but - toned down be - fore.

Move in Canon

Moving to show the shape of a melody is fun! Form three groups. **Perform** these movements in canon, as you sing "Old Abram Brown."

1 Crouch down for six beats.

2 Leap up on the word "more."

3 Slowly return to the starting position.

THINK! What are other ways you can move to show the shape of the melody of "Old Abram Brown"?

Play these parts on mallet instruments while the class sings the song.

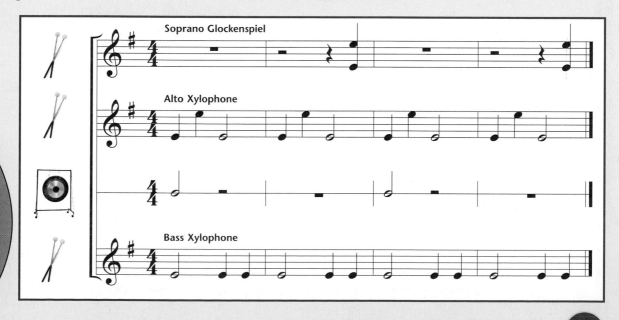

Soprano Glockenspiel

Alto Xylophone

Bass Xylophone

Melodies for the Night and Day

CONCEPT
MELODY
SKILLS
SING, READ, COMPOSE
LINKS
SOCIAL STUDIES, FINE ART

Sometimes it is a mystery how a song comes to us from a far-off country. The melody for "Allundé, Alluia." was an old harvest song from Nigeria, West Africa. People loved it so much it was sung in other parts of Africa, and the words changed. Now it has new life as a lullaby. Mothers sing their children to sleep with this song.

Sing "Allundé, Alluia." The melody uses the pitches of the pentatonic scale. **Read** the refrain using pitch syllables. Then sing the refrain in canon.

Allundé, Alluia

CD 2:20
Refrain
Gently Rocking

Melody based on a Nigerian Harvest Song
As sung and arranged by
Margaret Campbelle-Holman

Al - lun - dé, al - lun - dé._____ Al - lun - dé, al -
Pronunciation: a lʊn de a lʊn de   a lʊn de a

lu - ia._____ Al - lun - dé, al - lun - dé._____
lu ya   a lʊn de a lʊn de

3rd time go to Coda ✛   *End canon*

Al - lun - dé, al - lu - ia._____
a lʊn de a lu ya

Verse
mf

1. Jé pu wah yé_____ yé_____ ku - sah,
   ʒe pu wa ye   ye   ku sa
2. Man - dé a - qua - qua a - qua - qua man - dé,
   man de a kwa kwa a kwa kwa man de

Loving Embrace
Keith Mallet (b. 1948) created this painting in 1993. It shows a mother holding her child.

MAP

AFRICA

NIGERIA

Ai - yai - yai yé_____ al - lun - dé.____

ài yaì yaì ye   a lʊn de

𝄋 ***p*** *(for D.S.—**pp**)*

Ai - yai - yai yé_____ ai - yai - yé____ al - lun - dé.____

ài yaì yaì ye   ài yaì ye   a lʊn de

1.   *to Refrain* 2. *D.S. to 3rd ending* 3.   *to Refrain and Coda*

Coda

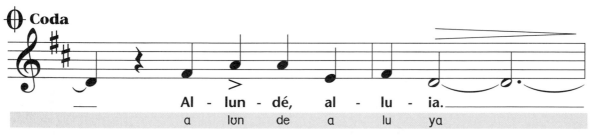

___ Al - lun - dé, al - lu - ia.____

a lʊn de a lu ya

p   ***pp***

___ Al - lun - dé, al - lu - ia.____

a lʊn de a lu ya

Crow and Sing!

Roosters really do crow when the sun comes up in the morning. You could even call them a farmer's alarm clock!

Sing "I'll Rise When the Rooster Crows."

I'll Rise When the Rooster Crows

CD 2:24

Appalachian Folk Song
As Sung by Uncle Dave Macon

I'll rise when the roos - ter crows.

I'll rise when the roos - ter crows.

I'm go - ing down south where the sun shines hot,

Down where the sug - ar - cane grows.

Something Worth Repeating

One kind of accompaniment is called an **ostinato**.

Ostinato is an Italian word that means stubborn. In music, an ostinato is stubborn because it repeats itself over and over!

Perform the ostinati below to accompany "I'll Rise When the Rooster Crows."

Create an Ostinato

Create your own ostinato. Fill two measures in $\frac{2}{4}$
Use these rhythms: ♩, ♫, ♩, and 𝄽
Play your ostinato on a percussion instrument as you sing "I'll Rise When the Rooster Crows."

Spotlight Your Success!

REVIEW

1 How many beats per measure are there in music in $\frac{2}{4}$ meter?

   a. 1   **b.** 3   **c.** 2   **d.** 4

2 Which pitches are in a pentatonic scale?

   a. *do re mi fa so la*

   b. *do re mi fa so*

   c. *do re mi so la*

   d. *do mi fa so*

3 What is the pitch around which a melody is centered?

   a. central pitch

   b. tonal center

   c. ostinato

   d. pitch syllable

READ AND LISTEN

1 **Read** these rhythms. Then listen. Which rhythm pattern do you hear?

   a.

   b.

   c.

2 **Read** these melody patterns using pitch syllables. Then **listen.** Which pattern do you hear?

a.

b.

c.

THINK!

1 What do you have to think about to be successful in singing a round?

2 **Describe** the ways that a roller coaster is similar to the contour of a melody.

3 Tell in your own words the meaning of the lyrics of "Something for Me, Something for You."

4 **Write** about your favorite song from this unit. What do you enjoy about it? How would you describe it to a friend?

CREATE AND PERFORM

1 Use ♩, ♩, ♫, and 𝄽 to fill four measures in 2/4 meter.

2 **Create** a melody by choosing pitches for your rhythm. Use pitches from the pentatonic scale in the key of C. End your melody on C.

3 **Sing** your melody using pitch syllables. Then play it on a mallet instrument.

4 **Perform** your melody for a friend.

Music News

Meet the Musician
ON NATIONAL RADIO!

Name: Abraham Feder
Age: 16
Instrument: Cello
Hometown: Chicago, Illinois

When Abraham Feder was two years old, all he wanted to do was to play his older brother's cello. "I'd ask my mom to let me play it, but every day she would say to me, 'Abe, don't touch your brother's cello!'"

Abe would not give up. Although his mother had told him not to touch his brother's cello, she never said he couldn't touch the bow. That gave Abe a great idea!

"I dragged out my father's 12-string guitar and grabbed my brother's cello bow," recalls Abe. "Then I sat on my bucket of stuffed bunnies, turned the guitar upright, and started playing it like a cello!" It wasn't long before Abe was given his very own real cello to play.

LISTENING CD 2:28

Sonata for Cello and Piano, Op. 40, Second Movement
by Dmitri Shostakovich

Listen to Abraham's performance and interview on the national radio program From the Top.

RECORDED INTERVIEW

Spotlight on the Saxophone

Careers

While earning a graduate degree as a bassoonist, Erika Kirsch learned the music library was separate from the university's main library. Her experience as an assistant there prepared her for a music librarian's career.

Conductors choose the music for their concerts, but music librarians work months before rehearsals start to get the music ready. Whether the performing group owns the music or needs to rent it, it has to be gathered. If it's copyrighted, permission fees must be paid. Making sure all players have special markings from the director or the same bowings for string players is also part of the job.

"You need to be a musician and know a lot about publishers, copyright law, and managing budgets," explains Ms. Kirsch. "It's never boring!"

Did You Know?

The saxophone, invented in 1846 by Adolphe Sax, is one of very few instruments named after its creator.

Although this single-reed instrument is considered a woodwind instrument, it is made of brass.

With its straight body, the soprano saxophone looks like a metal clarinet. Alto, tenor, and baritone saxophones have longer bodies that bend back up at the bottom and wider bells that curve out.

 LISTENING CD 3:1–2

Boléro (excerpt) by Maurice Ravel

Take Five (excerpt) by Paul Desmond

Listen to these two pieces for saxophone. Since the saxophone was invented in France, it is not surprising that many French composers, like Ravel, have used it in their music. The saxophone is also a favorite with jazz musicians. In "Take Five," a classic jazz piece in $\frac{5}{4}$ meter, you can hear its composer, Paul Desmond, on saxophone.

Musical Messages, Musical Journeys

Music is a special force in people's lives. You can express joy, love, hope, and sadness with music. When you share music with others, you are sending musical messages. In Unit 2 you will sing and play musical messages that will take you on journeys beyond your imagination.

Coming Attractions

Sing and play a popular song in Spanish.

Read a listening map of movie music.

Sing a call-and-response song.

What message does this song send?
Sing the song.

CD 3:4

Words and Music by Robert Bateman, Georgia Dobbins,
William Garrett, Freddie Gorman and Brian Holland

Oh yes, wait a min-ute, Mis-ter Post-man. Wait____

____ Mis-ter Post-man. Please Mis-ter Post-man, look and see,____

is there a let-ter in your bag for me?_ I've been wait-ing a

long, long time,_ since I heard from that friend of mine._

1. There must be some word to - day____
2. So man - y days____ you've passed me by,____

____ from my friend so far a - way._ Please, Mis-ter Post-man,
____ see the tears stand-in' in____ my eyes._ You did-n't stop to

CONCEPT
RHYTHM
SKILLS
SING, PERFORM, LISTEN
LINKS
FINE ART, LANGUAGE ARTS

Rhythm, Rhythm, Rhythm

The verses of "Frog Went A-Courtin'" tell a story. Some phrases have nonsense words that are fun to sing, but they may take practice!

Sing "Frog Went A-Courtin'" and enjoy the nonsense words.

Frog Went A-Courtin'

CD 3:7

Kentucky Folk Song
Additional Words by MMH

Verse

1. Frog went a - court - in' and he did ride.
(2.) rode right to Miss Mous - ie's door,
(3.) took Miss Mous - ie on his knee,
(4.) out my Un - cle Rat's con - sent,
5. Un-cle Rat laughed and shook his sides,

Rink - tum bod - y min - chy cam - bo.

Sword and buck - ler by his side,
Found Miss Mous - ie sweep-in' the floor.
And said, "Miss Mous-ie, will you mar - ry me?"
I could not mar-ry the pres - i - dent."
To think his niece would be a bride.

Rink - tum bod - y min - chy cam - bo.

46

Perform the rhythm of verse 1 using body percussion.

- **Clap** every syllable of words that tell the story.

- **Pat** the rhythm of the nonsense words.

Refrain

Ki - man-ee - ro down to Cai - ro, Ki - man-ee - ro Cai - ro.

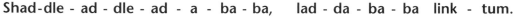

Shad-dle - ad - dle - ad - a - ba - ba, lad - da - ba - ba link - tum.

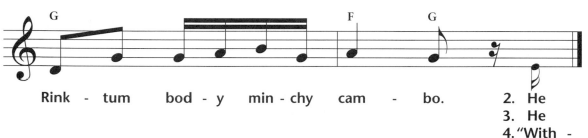

Rink - tum bod - y min - chy cam - bo.

2. He
3. He
4. "With -

6. Who will make the wedding gown?
   Old Miss Rat from Pumpkin Town.

7. Where will the wedding supper be?
   Way down yonder in a hollow tree.

8. What will the wedding supper be?
   A fried mosquito and black-eyed pea.

9. First to come was a bumblebee,
   He set his fiddle on his knee.

10. Next to come was a doodle bug,
    Carrying a water jug.

11. Next to come was a flying moth;
    She laid out the tablecloth.

12. Next to come was an itty-bitty flea
    To dance a jig for the bumblebee.

13. Next to come was a big old cow;
    She wanted to dance but she
        didn't know how.

14. Next to come was a big black snake;
    He ate up all the wedding cake.

15. Last to come was an old gray cat;
    She swallowed up the mouse and
        ate up the rat.

16. Mr. Frog went hopping over the
        brook;
    A duck came along and swallowed
        him up.

17. Now is the end of him and her;
    Guess there won't be no
        tadpoles covered with fur!

18. Little piece of cornbread lying on
        the shelf,
    If you want any more you can sing
        it yourself!

CONCEPT
MELODY

SKILLS
SING, PERFORM, ANALYZE

LINKS
SOCIAL STUDIES, DANCE

Early settlers of North America sang and danced when taking a break from their hard work. What do you do when taking a break from hard work?

"Cedar Swamp" is one song these pioneers would sing and dance to. **Sing** "Cedar Swamp."

Cedar Swamp

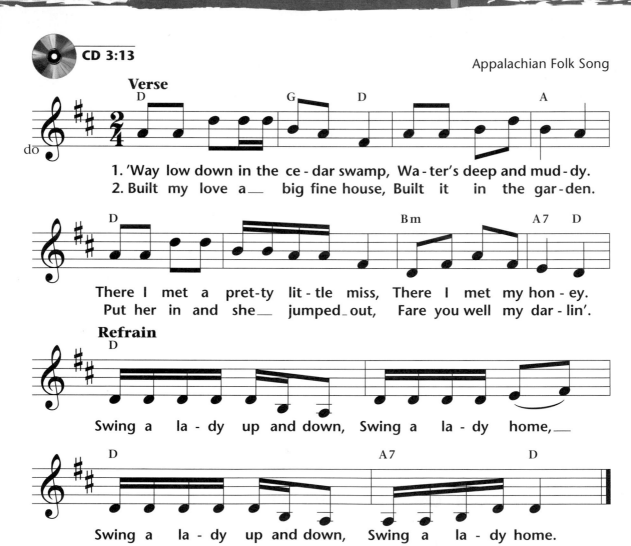

CD 3:13

Appalachian Folk Song

Verse

1. 'Way low down in the ce-dar swamp, Wa-ter's deep and mud-dy.
2. Built my love a— big fine house, Built it in the gar-den.

There I met a pret-ty lit-tle miss, There I met my hon-ey.
Put her in and she— jumped out, Fare you well my dar-lin'.

Refrain

Swing a la-dy up and down, Swing a la-dy home,—

Swing a la-dy up and down, Swing a la-dy home.

Identify the final pitch of "Cedar Swamp." This is the **tonal center** of the song. The tonal center is the pitch around which the melody of a song is built.

Dancing in a Longways Set

The dance formation you see below is called a longways set.
The pair of dancers at one end of the set is called the "head
couple." The pair at the other end is called the "foot."
Perform these movements as you sing "Cedar Swamp."

FORMATION

longways set

VERSE

right-elbow swing

For the verse, all couples
perform a right-elbow swing
and a left-elbow swing.

For the refrain, the head
couple gallops sideways
to the bottom of the set.

REFRAIN

gallop sideways

LESSON
3

CONCEPT
MELODY
SKILLS
LISTEN, SING,
IDENTIFY
LINKS
SOCIAL STUDIES

Lines or Spaces?

"**S**ail Away, Ladies" is a lively mountain dance tune. **Sing** the song.

Sail Away, Ladies

CD 3:20
Verse

Mountain Dance

1. Ain't no___ use to sit and cry;
2. I've got a home in Ten - nes - see,
3. If I ev - er get my new house done,   Sail a - way, la - dies,
4. Come a-long,___ boys, and go with me,
5. Hush lit - tle ba - by, don't you cry,

sail   a - way;

You'll be an an - gel by and by.
that's the___ place I wan - na be.
I'll give the old one to my son,
We'll go___ down to Ten - nes - see,
You'll be an an - gel by and by,

Refrain

Sail a - way, lad - ies, sail a - way. Don't you rock 'em

die - dy-o, don't___ you rock 'em die - dy-o, don't___ you rock 'em

die - dy - o, don't___ you rock 'em die - dy - o.

Pitches are written on a staff with 5 lines and 4 spaces. Both the spaces and lines are numbered from the bottom up.

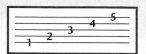

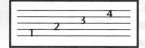

Lines of the staff   **Spaces of the staff**

Pitches can also be written below or above the lines.

This note is in the first space below the staff.   **This note is in the first space above the staff.**

When notes are higher or lower than the staff, they are written on lines above or below the staff. These lines are called **ledger lines**.

These notes are on ledger lines. What are the names of the notes on the ledger lines?

Where is *do* in this song? **Identify** the line or space where *do* is found.

When the word "ladies" is sung, notice that the pitches are lower than *do*. These pitches are called *low la* (*la₁*) and *low so* (*so₁*). What other word or words occur on *low la* or *low so* in the song?

 LISTENING / CD 3:23

Sail Away mountain dance

This recording features Malcolm Dalglish playing the hammered dulcimer.

Listen to "Sail Away." The hammered dulcimer has a unique sound. What instruments does it remind you of?

Mystery Musical Messages

CONCEPT
RHYTHM
SKILLS
CLAP, SING, LISTEN
LINKS
SOCIAL STUDIES

When you see music on a page, you may not know the rhythm right away. Think of the printed music as a message. Here are four steps that will help you decode a musical message.

1 **Speak** the rhythm of the song using jazz syllables. Say

- "dit" for ♩
- "doo wah" for ♫
- "dooby dooby" for ♬♬
- "doo dooby" for ♪♫
- "dooby doo" for ♫♪

2 **Clap** and speak the rhythm of the song.

3 **Sing** the song using jazz syllables.

4 **Sing** the song with the words.

Now try these four steps with "Early in the Morning" on the next page.

Sing "Early in the Morning at Eight O'Clock."

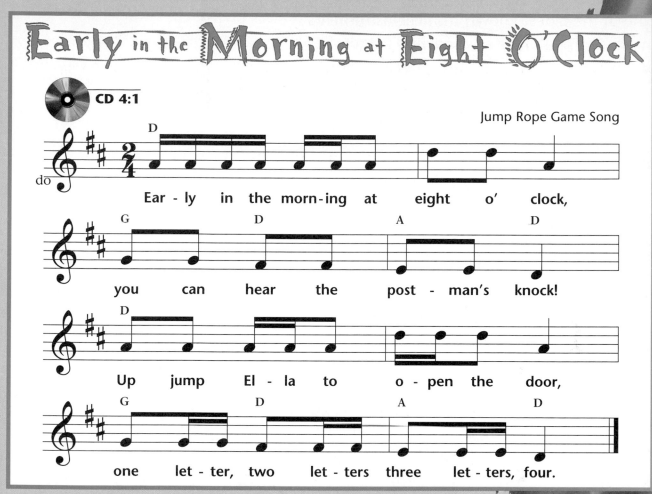

Early in the Morning at Eight O'Clock

CD 4:1

Jump Rope Game Song

Ear - ly in the morn-ing at eight o' clock,

you can hear the post - man's knock!

Up jump El - la to o - pen the door,

one let - ter, two let - ters three let - ters, four.

Four equal sounds to a beat can be written like this: 🎵
Play this accompaniment with "Early in the Morning at Eight O'Clock." **Identify** 🎵 each time it occurs.

Alto Glockenspiel

Bass Xylophone

Bass Metallophone

Flute Rhythms

One of the oldest known musical instruments is the flute. The flute is a woodwind instrument, or a wind instrument that is, or was originally, made of wood. At one time, flutes were made of wood, but today most flutes are made of metal. The sound of the flute is produced by blowing across a hole, like blowing across the mouth of a bottle.

Native American flute

Clap the first rhythm below and pat the second rhythm.

Create a musical conversation. Choose a partner. Perform these two rhythm patterns, then switch parts.

CD-ROM

Use *World Instruments* **CD-ROM** to learn more about flutes from all over the world.

Fife player in Colonial Williamsburg, Virginia

Flute player in South Africa

60

flute

Badinerie from Suite for Orchestra No. 2 in B Minor by Johann Sebastian Bach

"Badinerie" is a movement from the *Suite in B-minor* for solo flute and orchestra.

Listen for the rhythm that your group performed in this recording.

Meet the Musician

Johann Sebastian Bach (1685–1750) spent all of his life in Germany writing enormous amounts of music for organ, orchestra, solo instruments, choirs, and solo voices. As a church organist, he had to compose a new work for church services nearly every week. After his death, his music was almost forgotten. Yet today his music is widely performed and enjoyed around the world.

Mongolian flute ▶ player in New York, New York

Hmong flute player in traditional dress

CONCEPT
TONALITY
SKILLS
SING, LISTEN, PLAY
LINKS
HISTORY, SOCIAL STUDIES

Where's the Center?

"**L**a otra España" is a song about hope for freedom and a better life. This song is about life in the Americas when settlers came from Spain. **Sing** the song.

La otra España

The Other Spain

Juan Carlos Calderón
Arranged by Gilberto D. Soto
English Words by Linda Worsley

CD 4:5

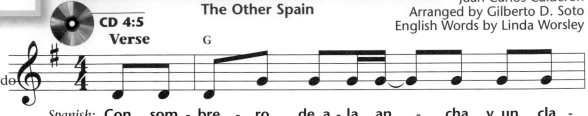

Verse

Spanish: Con som - bre - ro de a - la an - cha y un cla -
Pronunciation: kon som bre ro ðea la an cha iun kla -
English: With a wide-brimmed hat, a red__ car - na - tion

vel en la so - la - pa, un don Juan se hi - zo a la
βel en la so la pa un don xwan si soa la
tucked in his la - pel,__ a rov - ing sai - lor went to

mar. Con la tie - rra a sus es - pal - das la a - ven -
mar kon la tye ɾa sus es pal ðas la βen
sea. With the land be - hind his back,__ ad - ven - ture

tu - ra en su mi - ra - da su gui - ta - rra y un can -
tu ɾen su mi ɾa ða su gi ta ɾa i un kan
in his sight, he sang__ and played gui - ta - rra, and went to

tar. ¡Ay ma - ri - ne - ro,__ Ay ma - ri - ne -
tar o ma ɾi ne ɾo o ma ɾi ne
sea. Oh ma - ri - ne - ro!__ Oh, ma - ri - ne -

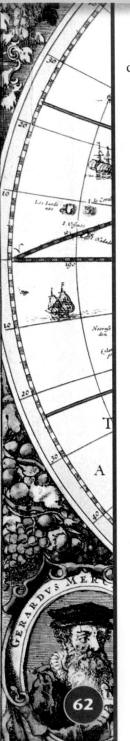

MAP
FRANCE
PORTUGAL
SPAIN
MOROCCO   ALGERIA

D7   G

-ro!__ De su ca-pa hi-zo un pon-cho de su gui-
ɾo   ðe su ka pa i soun pon cho ðe su gi
-ro!__ With his hood he made a cloak,__ and from his gui-

D7   G   C ⌐3⌐   D

ta-rra un cha-ran - go de su tie-rra   o-tra mar.
ta ɾa un cha ɾan   go ðe su tye ɾa   o tɾa maɾ
tar, a fine cha-ran - go, for his sing-ing   out at sea.

Refrain
G   C   D

Tú e - res la o - tra Es - pa - ña la que hue - le a ca-
tue ɾes la o tɾa es pa   nya la ke we lea ka
You   are "La o - tra Es - pa - ña," with your scent of car-

G   C   D   G   C

- ña, ta - ba - co y   brea;__   e - res la pe - re - zo-
nya ta βa ko i   βɾea   e ɾes la pe ɾe   so
- na - tions and su - gar   cane__   You, the ad - ven - tur - ous__

D   G   C   D

- sa la de piel do - ra - da, la ma - ri - ne - ra.__ Ah ah
sa la ðe pyel ðo ɾa   ða la ma ɾi ne   ɾa   a a
__ one with your eyes on the__ sea, La ma - ri - ne - ra!__ Ah, ah,

G   C   D7   G   C   D   G

ah ma - ri - ne - ra,__ ah ah ah ma - ri - ne - ra.__   Ah.
a ma ɾi ne   ɾa   a a   a ma ɾi ne   ɾa   a
ah, ma - ri - ne - ra!__ Ah, ah ah, ma - ri - ne - ra.__   Ah.

Play and Listen

Play this accompaniment with the refrain of "La otra España."

Playalong

Listen to this version of "La otra España." How is this recording different from the version you sang?

LISTENING   CD 4:9

La otra España (The Other Spain) by Juan Carlos Calderón

Juan Carlos Calderón wrote this song for the band Mocedades.

Meet the Musician

Juan Carlos Calderón (b. 1936) was born in Spain, but has worked all over the world. Like the sailor in "La otra España," Calderón left his home to find success in other countries. As a songwriter, a record producer, and a bandleader, he has been making music for more than forty years. He has written hits for Latin stars like Ricky Martin, Luis Miguel, and the band Mocedades.

Over 300 years ago, people were taken from their homes in Africa to the United States against their will. These enslaved people sang songs that expressed their longing for freedom, their homeland, and a better life. Such songs are called **spirituals**.

Sing the spiritual "'Most Done Ling'rin' Here." How is the tonal center of "'Most Done Ling'rin' Here" different from the tonal center of "La otra España"?

CD 4:10

African American Spiritual

'Most Done Ling'rin' Here

If you get there be-fore I do, 'Most done ling-'rin' here.

Look out for me I am com-in' too, 'Most done ling-'rin' here.

I'm go-in' a-way, go-in' a-way, I'm 'most done ling-'rin' here.

I'm go-in' a-way to Ga-li-lee, and I'm 'most done ling-'rin' here.

THINK! How do you think this song would give someone hope for a better life?

CONCEPT
FORM
SKILLS
SING, LISTEN, PLAY
LINKS
SOCIAL STUDIES, CULTURE, FINE ART

"**H**ine Ma Tov" is a Hebrew song from Israel that speaks of hope for people to live together peacefully. **Sing** the song.

Hine Ma Tov
How Good It Is

MAP
ISRAEL
GAZA
WEST BANK
JORDAN
EGYPT
SAUDI ARABIA

CD 4:13

Music by Allan E. Naplan
Words from Psalm 133:1

Refrain

Lai lai lai lai lai lai lai lai lai lai lai lai lai lai lai lai

Last time to Coda

Lai lai lai lai lai lai lai lai lai lai lai lai lai lai lai lai

Verse

Hebrew: ה - נֵ מָ נֵה - טוֹב - וּ מָה - שְׁ‑עִים בְּט‑אַ חִים‑גַּם יָ -

Pronunciation: hi   ne ma tov u   ma na yim she vet a xim gam ya

English: **How** good it is for all of us to join to-geth-er in

Groups of phrases make up **sections** of songs. Sections are labeled with capital letters. The first section is A, the next B, and so on.

Look at the song. **Identify** the form of "Hine Ma Tov."

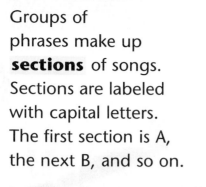

THINK! **Describe** the difference between the A and B sections of "Hine Ma Tov."

Gm		B♭	C	F		Dm	

חַד - הִ - נֵה מַה טוֹב וּ - מַה נָּ - עִים שֶׁ - בֶּ
xad hi ne ma tov u ma na yim she vet

song. Let our voi - ces raise with songs of praise that we'll

Go back to the beginning.
Last time to refrain then Coda

1. B♭ ... C 7 **2.** B♭ ... C 7 ... F

אַ - חִים גַּם יָ - חַד הִ - אַ - חִים גַּם יָ - חַד
a xim gam ya xad hi a xim gam ya xad

sing the whole day long. How sing the whole day long.

Coda

Dm		B♭	C 7	F	

שֶׁ - בֶּ אַ - חִים גַּם יָ - חַד
she vet a xim gam ya xad

That we'll sing the whole day long.

Happy Go Lucky!

Music has the power to make you happy and helps you forget your troubles. In Unit 3 you will sing and play music from all over the world that will make you feel good inside! How does music make you happy?

Coming Attractions

Sing a song from the Philippines.

Create harmony for a cowboy song.

Play chords to accompany an Israeli folk song.

"Happy Talk" is a song from the Broadway musical *South Pacific*.

Sing "Happy Talk." What do you think the words mean?

CD 5:8

Music by Richard Rodgers
Words by Oscar Hammerstein II

Refrain

Hap - py Talk, keep talk - in' Hap-py Talk._____

Talk a-bout things you'd like to do._____ You

got to have a dream.__ If you don't have a dream,__

how you gon - na have a dream__ come true?

Rhythms on the Railway

CONCEPT
RHYTHM

SKILLS
LISTEN, SING,
READ, PRACTICE

LINKS
SOCIAL STUDIES,
MOVEMENT,
THEATRE

By the middle of the 1800s, railroads in the United States were being built to connect the eastern and western states. "Pat Works on the Railway" is a song about an Irishman who worked on these railroads.

Listen to the recording as you read the words of the song.

Sing "Pat Works on the Railway."

Pat Works on the Railway

CD 5:11

American Railroad Song

1. In eight - een hun - dred and for - ty - one, I
2. In eight - een hun - dred and for - ty - two, I
3. In eight - een hun - dred and for - ty - three, 'twas
4. It's "Pat, do this," ___ and "Pat, do that," with -

put me cord - 'roy breech - es on, I put me cord - 'roy
left the old world for the new, 'Twas sor - ry luck that
then I met sweet Bid-dy Ma - gee, And an el-e - gant wife she's
out a stock - ing or cra - vat, And noth - ing but an

breech - es on to work up - on the rail - way.
brought me through to work up - on the rail - way.
been to me while work - in' on the rail - way.
old straw hat while work - in' on the rail - way.

Say the phrase "Fil-li-me-oo-re-i-re-ay."

| Fil- | li- | me- | oo- | re- | i- | re- | ay |

Which syllables have three equal sounds per beat?

Which syllables have two unequal sounds per beat?

Which syllable has one sound per beat?

Practice saying and clapping these words.

• Three equal sounds per beat

| **Fil-** | **li-** | **me-** | **Fil-** | **li-** | **me-** | **Fil-** | **li-** | **me-** | **Fil-** | **li-** | **me-** |

• Two unequal sounds per beat

| **oo-** | **re-** | **i-** | **re-** | **oo-** | **re-** | **i-** | **re-** |

• One sound per beat

| **ay** | **ay** | **ay** | **ay** |

Read the following rhythms using the words you practiced above.

Refrain

Em   G

Fil - li - me - oo - re - i - re-ay,   Fil - li - me-oo - re - i - re-ay,

Em   Am   Em

Fil - li - me - oo - re - i - re-ay, To work up-on the rail - way.

March to the Beat

"Macnamara's Band" is a song about an Irish marching band.

Pat with the beat as you sing the song.

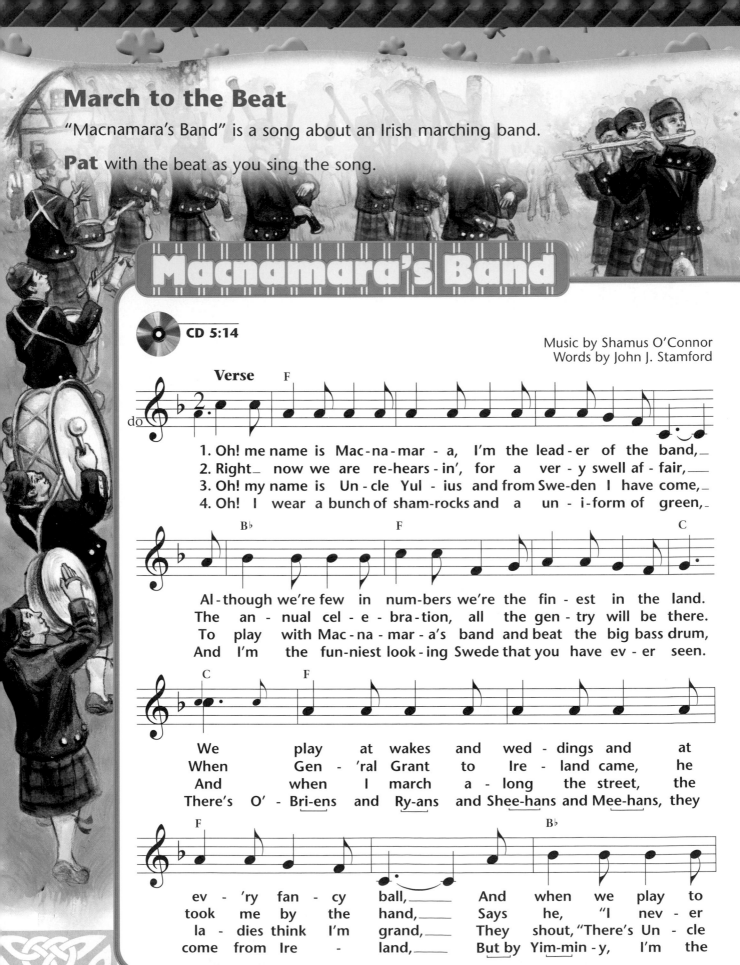

Macnamara's Band

CD 5:14

Music by Shamus O'Connor
Words by John J. Stamford

Verse

F

1. Oh! me name is Mac-na-mar-a, I'm the lead-er of the band,_
2. Right_ now we are re-hears-in', for a ver-y swell af-fair,___
3. Oh! my name is Un-cle Yul-ius and from Swe-den I have come,_
4. Oh! I wear a bunch of sham-rocks and a un-i-form of green,_

B♭   F   C

Al-though we're few in num-bers we're the fin-est in the land.
The an-nual cel-e-bra-tion, all the gen-try will be there.
To play with Mac-na-mar-a's band and beat the big bass drum,
And I'm the fun-niest look-ing Swede that you have ev-er seen.

C   F

We play at wakes and wed-dings and at
When Gen-'ral Grant to Ire-land came, he
And when I march a-long the street, the
There's O'-Bri-ens and Ry-ans and Shee-hans and Mee-hans, they

F   B♭

ev-'ry fan-cy ball,___ And when we play to
took me by the hand,___ Says he, "I nev-er
la-dies think I'm grand,___ They shout, "There's Un-cle
come from Ire-land,___ But by Yim-min-y, I'm the

88

Rhythms o' the Irish Band

"Macnamara's Band" uses many of the same rhythms as "Pat Works on the Railway."

Identify a word from the refrain of "Macnamara's Band" that has three equal sounds per beat.

Then, find words from the refrain that have two unequal sounds per beat. How about one sound per beat?

fu - ner - als,   we   play   the   march   from   Saul.
saw   the   likes   of   Mac - na - mar - a's   band."
Yul - ius   play - ing   with   an   I - rish   band."
on - ly   Swede   in   Mac - na - mar - a's   band.

Refrain F

Oh! the drums go bang, and the cym - bals clang, and the horns they blaze a -

way;___ Mc - Car - thy pumps the old ba - zoon while I the pipes do play;

And Hen - nes - sey Ten - nes - see too - tles the flute, and the mu - sic is some - thin'

grand;___ A cred - it to old Ire - land is Mac - na - mar - a's band.

Step, Skip, Leap into Calypso

CONCEPT
MELODY
SKILLS
SING, LISTEN,
READ, PLAY
LINKS
MOVEMENT,
THEATER,
VISUAL ARTS

"**W**ater Come a Me Eye" is a calypso song from Jamaica, an island nation in the Caribbean Sea.

Sing the song. Trace the shape of the melody with your finger as you sing.

MAP
THE BAHAMAS
CUBA
JAMAICA HAITI PUERTO RICO
DOMINICAN REPUBLIC

Water Come a Me Eye

CD 5:17

Calypso Jamaican Song
Arr. by Marjery Hargest Jones

Verse

1. Ev - 'ry time I think of Li - za,
2. Don't know why you went a - way,— } Wa-ter come_ a me eye.
3. Time go slow when love is past,—
4. Lis - ten 'cause I'm call - in' you,—

Ev - 'ry time I think of Li - za,
When you com - in' home to stay?_ } Wa-ter come_ a me eye.
When you come back, time go fast,—
And my heart is call - in' too,—

Refrain

Come back Li - za, come back girl, Wa - ter come_ a me eye.

1., 2., 3. | 4.

Come back Li - za, come back girl, Wa - ter come_ a me eye. eye.

90

Melodies can move in many ways. Look at the examples below from "Water Come a Me Eye."

Some melodies have **repeated notes**. They stay on the same pitch.

Ev-   'ry time I
▬▬▬▬   ▬▬   ▬▬   ▬▬▬

Melodies can move by **steps**. They move by going to the next higher or lower pitch.

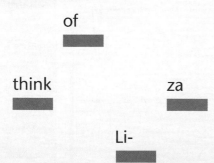

            me
        a   ▭▭ eye
    come ▭   ▭▭▭▭
  ter ▭
Wa- ▭▭
  ▭

When a melody moves by **skips**, it moves higher or lower by jumping over one pitch. When it moves by leaps it jumps over more than one pitch.

      of
    ▬▬▬

think   za
▬▬▬   ▬▬▬

        Li-
        ▬▬▬

Step Over to South America

Listen to the recording. The melody in the first section of the song uses many repeated notes. How does the melody in the second section of the song move?

 LISTENING CD 5:20

One Note Samba
by Antonio Carlos Jobim

"One Note Samba" is a song from Brazil about a melody built on one pitch. The piece has two sections.

Read the rhythms below.

Play along with "One Note Samba" on classroom instruments as you listen to the recording again.

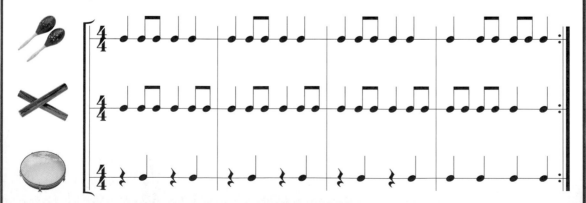

Playalong

Candombe played in the streets of Montevideo, Uruguay

Listen to *Repicados sobre Madera* for each of the different drums. How can you tell the three drums apart?

🔘 **LISTENING** CD 5:21

Repicados sobre Madera (excerpt) Uruguayan candombe

This recording features drummers from Uruguay.

Learn About Candombe

Candombe is a type of music from Uruguay, a country in South America that borders Brazil and Argentina. Candombe is based on a rhythm brought by enslaved people from Africa to Uruguay over two hundred years ago. The rhythm is played by three types of drums: *tambor piano, tambor chico,* and *tambor repique.* Because each drum is a different size, each drum is also a different pitch. Candombe is played on the streets of Montevideo, the capital of Uruguay. It is also played for carnivals and festivals.

◀ Drums played in a parade in Montevideo

CONCEPT
MELODY

SKILLS
SING, READ, LISTEN

LINKS
LANGUAGE ARTS, MOVEMENT, VISUAL ARTS

"**L**ove Somebody" is a song that features many of the pitch syllables you already know. **Name** the pitch syllables you know.

Sing the song. Find the new pitch.

American Folk Song

1. Love some-bod-y, yes I do. Love some-bod-y, yes I do.
2. Love some-bod-y, can't guess who. Love some-bod-y, can't guess who.

Love some-bod-y, yes I do. Love some-bod-y but I won't tell who.
Love some-bod-y, can't guess who. Love some-bod-y but I won't tell who.

Love some-bod-y, yes I do. Love some-bod-y, yes I do.

Love some-bod-y, yes I do. And I hope some-bod-y loves me too.

There are five pitches in the melody for the A section of "Love Somebody." These are four of the pitches:

do   re   mi   so

The melody has a pitch between *so* and *mi*. It is called *fa*. In this song, *so* and *mi* are on lines and *fa* is on the space between them.

do   re   mi   fa   so

On what words do you sing *fa* in "Love Somebody"?

Read the song with pitch syllables and hand signs.

Read the poem below. How is "Whispers" similar to the lyrics of "Love Somebody"?

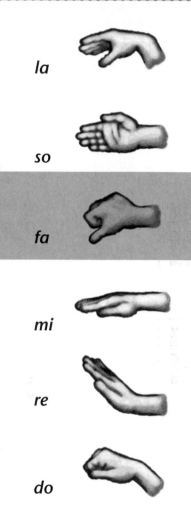

la

so

fa

mi

re

do

Whispers

Whispers
      tickle through your ear
      telling things you like to hear.
Whispers
      are soft as skin
      letting little words curl in.
Whispers
      come so they can blow
      secrets others never know.

—*Myra Cohn Livingston*

Moving to a New Key

Whatever pitch *do* is on, all of the other pitches of the scale move with it.

Sing the first five pitches of the scale when *do* is G.

do re mi fa so

alto recorder ▶

- Where is *do*?
- Where is *mi*?
- Where is *so*?
- Where is *fa*?

Below is the melody of the A section of "Contredanse" by the French composer Jean-Philippe Rameau.

Read the melody above using pitch syllables and hand signs.

Meet the Musician

Jean-Philippe Rameau (1680–1764) was a French musician and composer. While working as an organist, he wrote one of the most important books in Western music about harmony. When Rameau was fifty years old, he began writing operas. They were so popular in Paris that he continued to write more of them until he was eighty years old.

Meet the Recorder

The recording below of "Contredanse" includes recorders. The recorder is a woodwind instrument that was popular in Europe during the 1500s and 1600s. A consort is a group of the same instruments in different sizes.

Listen to the recording. How many times do you hear the A section?

 LISTENING CD 5:26

▲tenor recorder

soprano recorder ▲

Contredanse from *Les Indes galantes* (excerpt)
by Jean-Philippe Rameau

"Contredanse" was written in the 1700s. It is from one of Rameau's most famous operas, *Les Indes galantes* (*The Gallant Indies*).

Follow the listening map below of the B, C, and D sections for "Contredanse."

bass recorder ▶

Listening Map for Contredanse

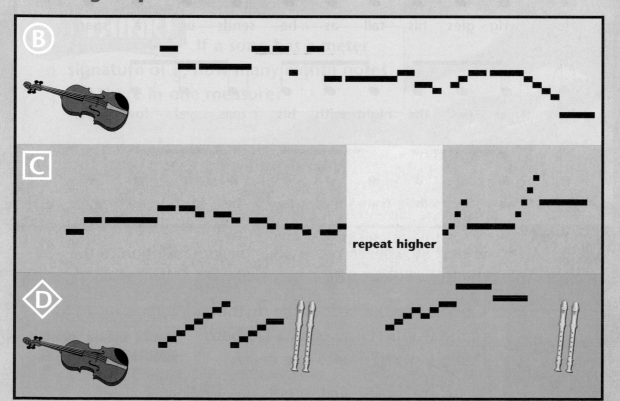

repeat higher

San Juan Rhythms

In "La sanjuanerita," a young girl tells about living in San Juan, Guatemala. **Identify** the meter signature for the song. Then, find these two rhythm patterns in "La sanjuanerita."

Sing the song.

MAP

MEXICO

HONDURAS

GUATEMALA

NICARAGUA

La sanjuanerita
The Girl from San Juan

CD 6:1

Words and Music by Guadalupe Hernández
English Words by Linda Worsley

Spanish: U - na chi - qui - lla de San Juan, quie-re a su pue-blo que es un jar-
Pronunciation: u na chi ki ya ðe san xwan kye rea su pwe βlo kes un xar
English: **There is a girl from old San Juan, she loves her town, a gar - den**

dín, con flo-re - ci - tas de tem-po ral li-rios, cla - ve - les y a-lhe-
ðin kon flo re si tas ðe tem po ral li ryos kla βe les ia le
fair, col-or-ful i - ris bloom in the spring, lil - ies and bright car-na-tions

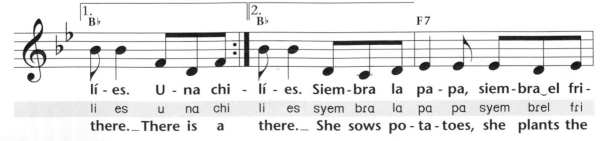

lí - es. U - na chi - lí - es. Siem-bra la pa - pa, siem-bra el fri-
li es u na chi li es syem bra la pa pa syem brel fri
there.__There is a there.__ She sows po - ta-toes, she plants the

100

Tejedoras

This painting by Antonio Coché Mendoza (b. 1953) illustrates weavers practicing their trade in San Juan, Guatemala.

jol. Bue-na co - se-cha_el cam - po le - da. Y en la

xol bwe na ko se chel kam po le ða i en la

beans, boun-ti - ful har - vest comes from the fields. Then comes fi -

fies-ta de San Juan, se po-ne_a-le - gre su co-ra-zón. Con la ma-

fyes ta ðe san xwan se po nea le gɾe su ko ɾa son kon la ma

es - ta in San Juan, Her heart is light and joy-ful a - gain, to the ma-

rim - ba van a bai - lar to - dos con - ten - tos un buen son.

ɾim ba βan a βai laɾ to ðos ko ten tos un βwen son

rim - ba, now she will dance, all are con - tent and hap - py then!

CONCEPT
METER

SKILLS
IDENTIFY, PAT, PLAY, LISTEN

LINKS
CULTURES, SOCIAL STUDIES

"Sitsiritsit" is a traditional song from the Philippines. The word "sitsiritsit" represents the sound of a rooster crowing. **Sing** the song with the Tagalog words. Find the insect names for butterfly *(alibangbang)*, firefly *(salaginto)*, and beetle *(salagubang)*.

MAP
CHINA
VIETNAM
PHILIPPINES
MALAYSIA
INDONESIA

Sitsiritsit

CD 6:5

Traditional Tagalog Song

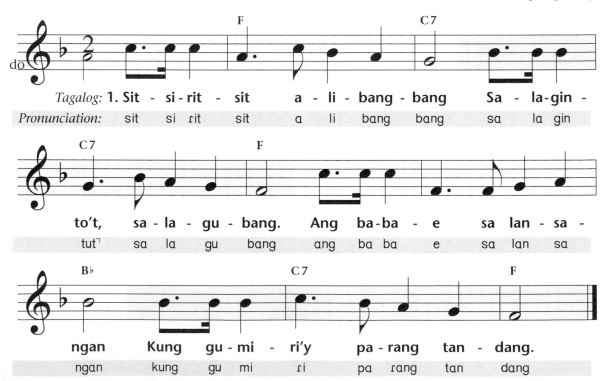

Tagalog: 1. Sit - si - rit - sit a - li - bang - bang Sa - la - gin -

Pronunciation: sit si rit sit a li bang bang sa la gin

to't, sa - la - gu - bang. Ang ba - ba - e sa lan - sa -

tut sa la gu bang ang ba ba e sa lan sa

ngan Kung gu - mi - ri'y pa - rang tan - dang.

ngan kung gu mi ri pa rang tan dang

Pat with the beat as you sing the song. Is the beat in groups of 2 or groups of 3?

The $\frac{2}{2}$ meter signature means that there are two beats per measure and the $\downarrow$ gets one beat. $\frac{2}{2}$ can also be written like this: $\frac{2}{2}$

Play the parts below on mallet instruments and finger cymbals as you sing the song.

Dancing the *Tinikling*

The national dance of the Philippines is called the *Tinikling*. The dancers copy the movements of the tikling birds (similar to herons or cranes).

Tinikling originated in Leyte, one of the Visayan Islands. It is located in the middle of the country. The Spaniards took control of the Philippines in the 1500s. They forced the native Filipinos to work in the rice fields. Slower workers were rapped on the feet with bamboo poles as punishment. The workers would jump around the poles so they would miss them. This is how the dance was created.

Global Voices

bandurria

laud

Filipinos dancing the Tinikling

Listen to *Tinikling*. **Pat** the beat as you listen.
Is the beat in groups of 2 or groups of 3?

 LISTENING CD 6:9

Tinikling national dance of the Philippines

Native Filipinos do not usually sing along
when dancing *Tinikling*. It is accompanied
by a rondalla, an orchestra of plucked string
instruments. These instruments are the
bandurria, laud, octavina, guitar, and the
bajo de uñas.

octavina

▼ **These Filipino women are part of a parade in The Philippines.**

guitar

bajo de uñas

The Loud and Soft of It!

CONCEPT
DYNAMICS

SKILLS
SING, IDENTIFY,
COMPARE, LISTEN

LINKS
SOCIAL STUDIES,
CULTURES

Loudness and softness make music expressive. **Dynamics** refers to the loudness and softness of music. Dynamic markings in music show how loud or soft it should be performed. Read the chart below to learn about the different dynamic markings.

ff	*fortissimo*	very loud
f	*forte*	loud
mf	*mezzo forte*	medium loud
mp	*mezzo piano*	medium soft
p	*piano*	soft
pp	*pianissimo*	very soft
<	*crescendo*	gradually get louder
>	*decrescendo*	gradually get softer

Sing "El manisero," a song originally from Cuba.

Identify the dynamic markings in the song.

El manisero

Peanut Vendor

CD 6:10

Music and Spanish Words by Moises Simons
English Words by Linda Worsley

Spanish: ¡Ma-ní!___ ¡Ma-ní!___ Ca-se-ri-ta no te_a
Pronunciation: ma ni ma ni ka se ɾi ta no tea
English: Ma-ní!___ Ma-ní!___ Come a-long and buy them,

cues-tes a___ dor-mir, sin co-mer te_un cu-cu-ru-cho de_ ma-ní.
kwes tes a ðoɾ miɾ sin ko meɾ teun ku ku ɾu cho ðe ma ni
don't lie down_ to sleep. You can buy a cone of ma-ní, good_ to eat.

Dynamics on the High Seas

Listen for the expressive changes in dynamics as the orchestra plays "Guadalcanal March," from *Victory at Sea*.

 **LISTENING** | CD 6:14

Guadalcanal March from *Victory at Sea*
by Richard Rodgers

Richard Rodgers was asked to create the music for *Victory at Sea*, a documentary film about World War II.

Meet the Musician

Richard Rodgers (1902–1979) is one of the most famous composers of American musicals. He wrote many of these for Broadway, including *Oklahoma!*, *The King and I*, and *South Pacific*. Many of his musicals were turned into Hollywood movies.

THINK! Imagine a performance of "Guadalcanal March" with no changes in dynamics. **Compare** with the version you heard. Which do you like better? Why?

Read the listening map below as you listen to the recording again.

Listening Map for Guadalcanal March from *Victory at Sea*

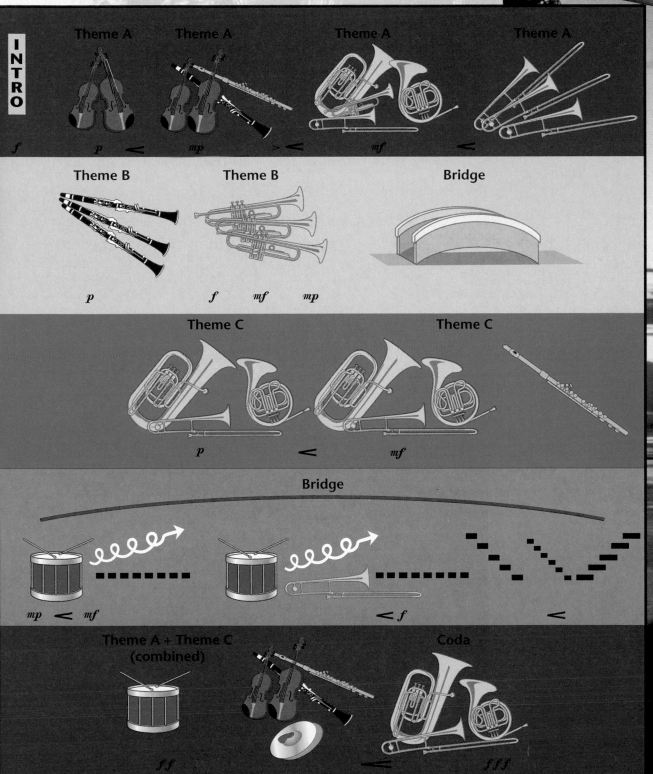

INTRO

Theme A Theme A Theme A Theme A
f *p* < *mp* > < *mf* <

Theme B Theme B Bridge
p *f* *mf* *mp*

Theme C Theme C
p < *mf*

Bridge
mp < *mf* < *f* <

Theme A + Theme C (combined) Coda
ff < *fff*

Round Up the Key

CONCEPT
HARMONY
SKILLS
SING, PLAY,
LISTEN
LINKS
MOVEMENT,
SOCIAL STUDIES,
CULTURES

The **key signature** at the beginning of a song indicates the key of a given piece of music. In "Night Herding Song" the key signature has one **flat** (♭) on the third line. The flat comes before the meter signature. It tells you that this note is flat throughout the piece of music.

This key signature also tells you that *do* is in the first space. What is the letter name for *do*?

"Night Herding Song" is a cowboy song. *Do* is the tonal center for the song. One group will sing the tonal center *do*, while the other group sings the song.

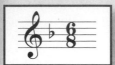

Night Herding Song

CD 6:15

Cowboy Song

1. Oh say, lit - tle do - gies, quit
2. Oh, lay down, my do - gies, quit

rov - ing a - round. You've wan - dered and tram - pled all
shift - ing a - round. Just stretch a - way out on the

o - ver the ground. Oh, graze a - long, do - gies, and
big, o - pen ground. My horse is leg - wea - ry and

Harmony in the Corral

Singing or playing two pitches at the same time creates **harmony**. Singing the tonal center with a song is one way to harmonize the melody. Now harmonize the song another way.

Sing this pattern with two pitches: *do* (F) and *low so* (C), while the rest of the class sings the song.

THINK! Which harmony sounded better to you? Why?

| move kind - a slow. | And don't be | for - ev - er so |
| I'm aw - ful tired. | If you get | a - way, then I'll |

| much on the go. | Move slow, lit - tle | do - gies, move |
| sure - ly be fired. | Oh, lay down, my | do - gies, lay |

slow.____ Hi - o, hi - o,____ hi - o.
down.____ Hi - o, hi - o,____ hi - o.

Harmony from Israel

"Achshav" ("Now") is a folk song from Israel. **Sing** the song with both the Hebrew and the English words.

Achshav

Now

CD 6:18

Israeli Folk Song

Building Chords

Chords are built by sounding three or more pitches together from the scale. The tonal center for "Achshav" is *do*. This song is harmonized using two chords, one built on *do* and one built on *so*.

The first chord is built on the first step of the scale, *do*. It is called the one, or "I," chord. It sounds these pitches together:

The second chord is built on the fifth step of the scale, *so*. This chord is called the five, or "V," chord. It sounds these pitches together:

Use the I chord and the V chord to accompany "Achshav" with the following rhythm pattern:

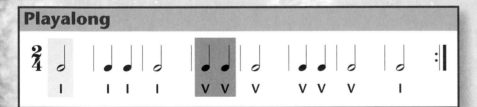

 Art Gallery

Valley of the Moon, Eilat

Judith Yellin Ginat (b. 1921) created this etching in 1968. It shows a valley in the Arava region of Israel.

CONCEPT
RHYTHM

SKILLS
SING, IDENTIFY,
READ, CREATE

LINKS
THEATER,
SOCIAL STUDIES

"**H**ey, Look Me Over"
is from the Broadway
musical, *Wildcat*.

Sing the song. **Identify**
all of the measures in "Hey,
Look Me Over" where there
are three equal sounds
(♪♪♪) on every beat.

From the original
Broadway production
of *Wildcat*

Hey, Look Me Over

CD 6:22

Music by Cy Coleman
Words by Carolyn Leigh

Hey look me o - ver, lend me an ear;
Up like a rose - bud, high on the vine;

Fresh out of clo - ver, mort - gaged up to
Don't turn up your nose, bud, take a tip from

1.

here._____ But don't pass the plate, folks,

don't pass the cup; I fig - ure when-ev - er you're

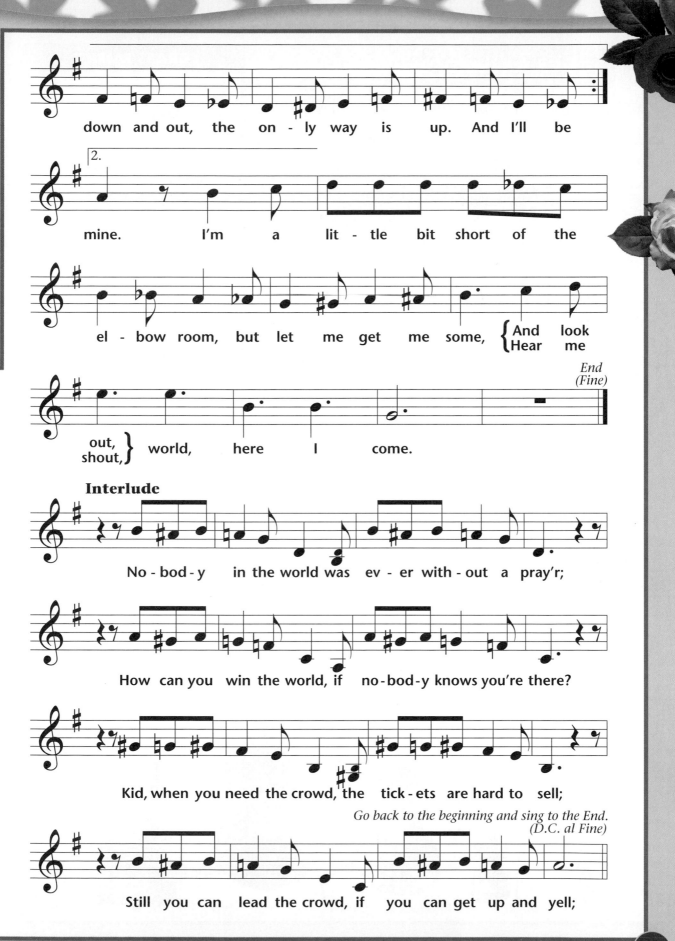

down and out, the on - ly way is up. And I'll be

2.

mine. I'm a lit - tle bit short of the

el - bow room, but let me get me some, { And look / Hear me

End (Fine)

out, / shout, } world, here I come.

Interlude

No - bod - y in the world was ev - er with - out a pray'r;

How can you win the world, if no - bod - y knows you're there?

Kid, when you need the crowd, the tick - ets are hard to sell;

Go back to the beginning and sing to the End.
(D.C. al Fine)

Still you can lead the crowd, if you can get up and yell;

Magical Rhythms on Magical Instruments

Create your rhythm accompaniment to play with "Hey, Look Me Over." **Use** ♩., ♩ ♪, and ♫♫ to fill four measures in $\frac{6}{8}$ meter.

 LISTENING CD 6:25

The Sorcerer's Apprentice (excerpt)
by Paul Dukas

This piece is an example of **program music**, which is music that tells a story.

Listen for the bassoon playing three equal sounds to a beat. What other instruments pictured here play this rhythm?

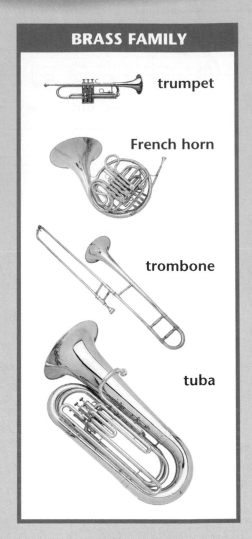

BRASS FAMILY

trumpet

French horn

trombone

tuba

STRING FAMILY

harp

double bass

cello

violin   viola

WOODWIND FAMILY

flute

piccolo

oboe

clarinet

English horn

alto saxophone

bassoon

PERCUSSION FAMILY

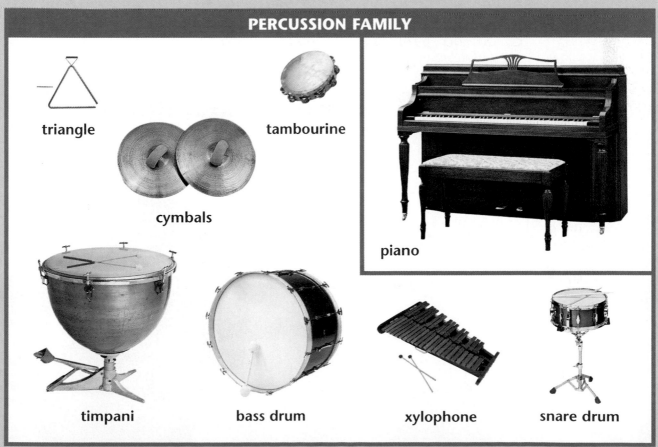

triangle

tambourine

cymbals

piano

timpani

bass drum

xylophone

snare drum

Spotlight Your Success!

REVIEW

1 What is a symbol that shows how many beats are in each measure and what kind of note equals one beat?

    a. meter signature   **b.** key signature   **c.** treble clef

2 Which rhythm has three equal sounds per beat in $\frac{6}{8}$ meter?

3 Which set of pitch syllables matches this melody?

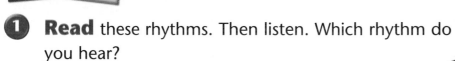

    a. *do do* | *so so* | *do do re re* | *do*

    b. *do do* | *la la* | *so so mi re* | *do*

    c. *do do* | *mi mi* | *fa mi re mi* | *do*

READ AND LISTEN

1 **Read** these rhythms. Then listen. Which rhythm do you hear?

    a.

    b.

    c.

    d.

2 **Read** these patterns using pitch syllables. Then listen.
Which pattern do you hear?

THINK!

1 How do you know whether a phrase is just beginning or is coming to an end?

2 How can you tell the difference between repeated notes, notes that move by step, and notes that move by leap?

3 Describe the different languages that you heard in this unit. Which language do you like best? Why?

4 **Write** about something you learned from the music, instruments, and cultures in the unit. If you could choose one song or dance to perform again, which would you choose? Why?

CREATE AND PERFORM

1 **Choose** ♪♪♪, ♩ ♪, and ♩. to fill four measures in $\frac{6}{8}$ meter.

2 **Practice** reading your rhythm.

3 **Play** your rhythm on a classroom instrument using two or more dynamics as you play.

Meet the Musician
ON NATIONAL RADIO!

Name: Neil Vasan
Age: 17
Instrument: Marimba
Hometown: Columbus, Ohio

Seventeen-year-old Neil Vasan plays both piano and marimba. His favorite time to practice is before he goes to bed at night. "This way, music provides a pleasant end to every day," he explains. Neil makes sure he takes a break in between practicing the two instruments, however. "If I don't, my arms cramp up from using them so much," he says.

Neil may want to be a professional musician one day. Then again, he may not.

Neil is also interested in chemistry and math, and he may decide to become a scientist. "I'm especially interested in organ transplantation," he states. "I think it's great that we are able implant an organ into another human being and the person can live as a result."

No matter what he decides to do for a career, Neil is certain he will always love playing music. "It is very hard to imagine my life without it!"

LISTENING CD 6:27–28

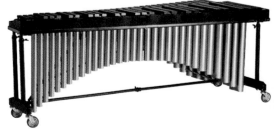

Concertino for Marimba, Op. 21, First Movement ("Vigorous") by Paul Creston

Listen to Neil's performance and interview on the national radio program **From the Top**.

RECORDED INTERVIEW

Spotlight on a Wind Quintet

Did You Know?

A wind quintet is made up of five instruments: flute, oboe, clarinet, French horn, and bassoon.

The players in a wind quartet sit in a semicircle. They need to see each other to carry on their musical conversations.

The French horn is the only brass instrument in the group. Its strong sound stands out clearly from the other instruments.

The quintet's highest notes can be played by the flute and the lowest notes usually come from the bassoon.

 LISTENING CD 6:29–30

Autumn Music, **First Movement (excerpt)** by Jennifer Higdon

Quintet, Op. 43, Menuet (excerpt) by Carl Nielsen

Listen to these two pieces for wind quintet. The five instruments have different voices, but can make a smooth, blended sound when they play together.

This song is from the musical *You're a Good Man, Charlie Brown*. It reminds you to think about the things that make you happy. How does music make you happy?

Sing the song.

The cast of the original Broadway production of *You're a Good Man, Charlie Brown*

Happiness

from the musical *You're a Good Man, Charlie Brown*

 CD 6:31

Words and Music by Clark Gesner

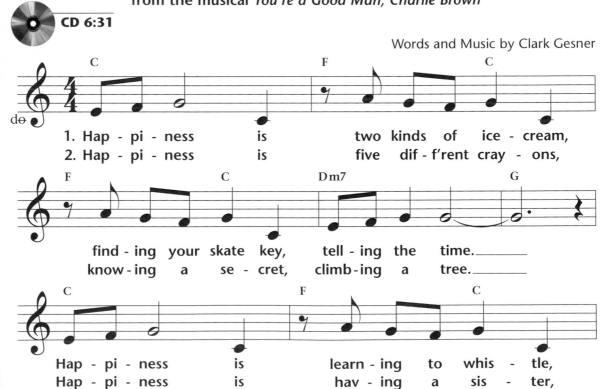

1. Hap - pi - ness   is   two kinds of ice - cream,
2. Hap - pi - ness   is   five dif - f'rent cray - ons,

find - ing your skate key,   tell - ing the time._____
know - ing a se - cret,   climb - ing a tree._____

Hap - pi - ness   is   learn - ing to whis - tle,
Hap - pi - ness   is   hav - ing a sis - ter,

ty - ing your shoes for the ver - y first time.____
shar - ing a sand - wich,___ get - ting a - long.____

Hap - pi - ness is play - ing the drum in your own school
Hap - pi - ness is sing - ing to - geth - er when day is

band, and hap - pi - ness is walk - ing hand in
through, and hap - pi - ness is those who sing with

hand. you. Hap - pi - ness is

morn - ing and eve - ning, day - time and night - time too. For

hap - pi - ness is an - y - one, and an - y - thing at

all that's loved by you.

LESSON
1

CONCEPT ▶
MELODY
SKILLS ▶
SING, IDENTIFY,
MOVE, PERFORM
LINKS ▶
CULTURES,
MATHEMATICS

Leap Over the Rainbow

Some songs put dreams and wishes into words.
What are the dreams and wishes in this song?
Sing "Over the Rainbow."

CD 7:1

Music by Harold Arlen
Words by E.Y. Harburg

Refrain

1. Some - where   o - ver the rain - bow   way   up   high,
2. Some - where   o - ver the rain - bow   skies   are   blue,
3. Some - where   o - ver the rain - bow   blue - birds   fly.

3rd time To Coda

there's   a   land   that   I   heard   of   once   in   a   lull - a -
and   the   dreams that you dare   to   dream real - ly   do   come
Birds   fly   o - ver the rain - bow,   why then, oh why can't

by.   true.   Some - day I'll wish up - on   a   star and

wake   up   where   the   clouds   are   far   be - hind   me.____

126

Think about how you move. Sometimes you take a step at a time. Sometimes it just feels great to take a flying leap! Melodies can move the same way. Sing "Over the Rainbow" again. **Identify** the melodic leaps in the song. **Move** to show the distance of the leap.

A whole note gets four beats in $\frac{4}{4}$ and looks like this: o

An eighth rest gets one half beat in $\frac{4}{4}$ and is written like this: ↯ Identify both of these in "Over the Rainbow."

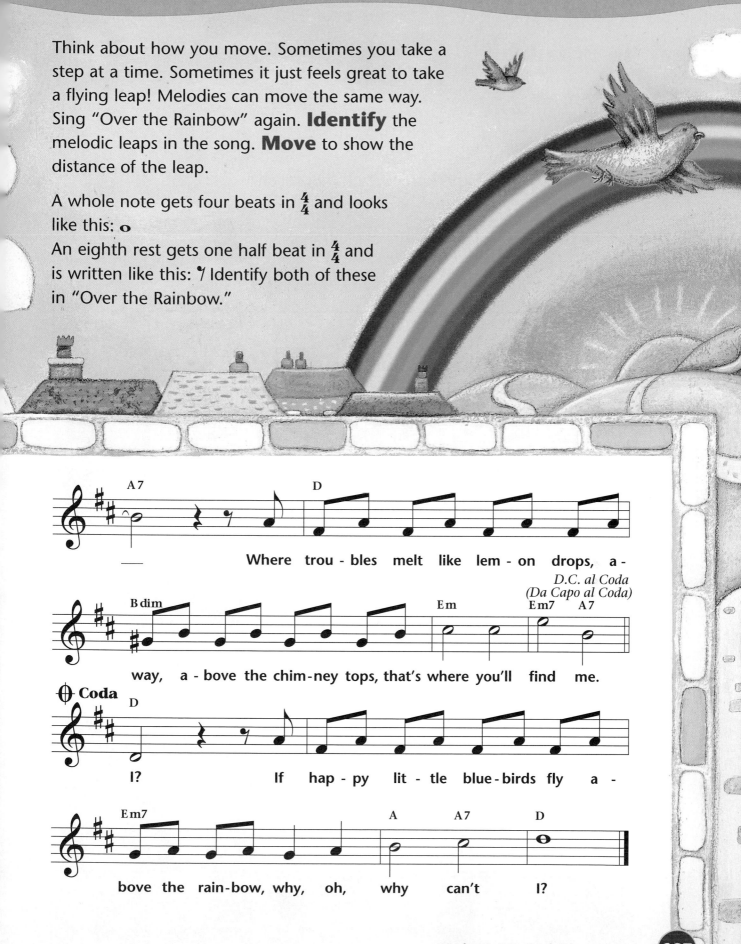

Where trou-bles melt like lem-on drops, a-

D.C. al Coda
(Da Capo al Coda)

way, a - bove the chim-ney tops, that's where you'll find me.

Coda

I? If hap-py lit-tle blue-birds fly a-

bove the rain-bow, why, oh, why can't I?

Leap to Brazil

 LISTENING CD 7:4

Oito Batutas by Pixinguinha

"Oito Batutas" is written and performed by the Brazilian composer Pixinguinha.

clarinet

Listen for the wide leaps played by the clarinet in the A section of "Oito Batutas."

Meet the Musician

Pixinguinha (1898–1973), whose given name was Alfredo da Rocha Vianna, Jr., was a composer from Brazil who played the flute and saxophone. He is known as one of the founding fathers of samba. Pixinguinha was considered a pioneer for Brazilian music, touring South America and Europe.

Playing Octaves

An **octave** leap is a wide leap. An octave is the distance between two pitches that have the same names. Find pitches that are an octave apart on the xylophone below.

Play the parts below on mallet instruments to practice playing octaves.

THINK!

What do you think the number eight has to do with an octave?

The Long and Short of It

CONCEPT
RHYTHM
SKILLS
SING, LISTEN, WRITE, PLAY
LINKS
VISUAL ARTS, LANGUAGE ARTS, CULTURES

The story of Noah's Ark tells about a man named Noah who prepared for a great flood by building an ark. When the rain started, Noah and his family loaded the ark with animals and watched as the floodwaters got higher and higher. After forty days and forty nights, the rain stopped and Noah and his animals were free to walk the land again.

Sing this song about Noah and his ark as you pat the beat. Then sing the song again as you clap the rhythm of the words. **Listen** to how the rhythm and beat fit together.

Old Ark's A-Moverin'

CD 7:5

African American Spiritual

A Freely
Refrain

Old Ark's a - mov-er - in', a - mov-er - in', a - mov-er - in'. The

Old Ark's a - mov - er - in' and I'm go - in' home.

End (Fine)

Art Gallery

Noah's Ark

This painting was created by Edward Hicks (1780–1849) in 1846. *Noah's Ark* illustrates the story described in "Old Ark's A-Moverin'."

B) Verse

G   D   G   D

1. Old Ark she reel,   Old Ark she rock,
2. How ma - ny days did the wa - ter_____ fall?
3. Old Ark she reel,   Old Ark she rock,

Go back to the beginning and sing to the End.
(D.C. al Fine)

G   D   A7   D

Old Ark land - ed on a moun-tain top.____
For - ty days__ and__ nights in all.____
Old Ark land - ed on a moun-tain top.____

THINK!

Read the lyrics "Old Ark's A-Moverin'" and look at the painting above. Sing the song again and think about the music. Do you think that the music expresses the lyrics? **Write** a short paragraph explaining why or why not.

Searching for Short-Long-Short

The short-long-short pattern in "Old Ark's A Moverin'" is two beats long. **Clap** this four-beat rhythm that starts with the short-long-short pattern.

Old Ark she reel,   Old Ark she rock,

Find the short-long-short pattern in the rhythm below, then clap the phrase.

Come now and join us, it's danc- ing day!

Perform this rhythm pattern as you sing "Peasant's Dancing Day," a folk song from the Balkans region of Eastern Europe.

Peasant's Dancing Day

CD 7:8

Balkan Folk Melody
Arranged by Ralph E. Marryott

Gm   D 7 Gm   F

Come now and join us, it's danc - ing day!

B♭   E♭   B♭ D 7 Gm   D 7

Come now and join us, it's danc - ing day!

Hear the fid-dles play-ing, see the danc-ers sway,

Come now and join us, it's danc-ing day!

slow to the end

Come now and join us, it's danc-ing day!

Unit 4 Musical Discoveries

Singing a New Note

CONCEPT
MELODY
SKILLS
SING, READ, PLAY
LINKS
CULTURES, SOCIAL STUDIES

CD-ROM

Use **World Instruments CD-ROM** to learn more about Chinese instruments.

In Asia, bamboo has always been an important part of art, culture, and everyday life. The *dizi* is a traditional Chinese flute made from bamboo with six holes and tuned to a major scale. The *dizi* has a shrill, buzzing sound when it is played.

"Bamboo Flute" is a song from China that is sung in Mandarin. **Sing** the song. Where is the new note?

dizi

MAP

RUSSIA

MONGOLIA

KOREA

CHINA

INDIA

JAPAN

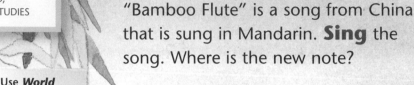

Bamboo Flute

CD 7:11

Collected by Kathy B. Sorensen
English Words by Linda Worsley

Pronunciation: yi gən tsə dru jə miɑu miɑu

English: **One straight pur - ple stick,   one stick of bam - boo,**

sung gei bɑu bɑu tsuɔ guɑn shɑu

Make a flute and play it, too._____

The pitches for the first phrase of "Bamboo Flute" are shown below, arranged from lowest to highest. The highest pitch is *high do (do¹)*. High do (do¹) is an octave above *do*. **Identify** *high do (do¹)* in the song. Sing the pitch syllables for this scale.

do re mi so la do¹

Read the first four lines of "Bamboo Flute" using pitch syllables.

shau ər due jʌng kou   kou ər due jʌng shau
When the flute is done,   You can make it sing,

shau juŋ tre tru shʊ shin diau
Put it to your mouth, Let the mu - sic ring.

shau bau bau yi di yi di shyɛ xue liau
What will it say? "Vi di vi di" loud and strong.

shau bau bau yi di yi di shyɛ xue liau
What will it play? "Vi di vi di" hear the song.____

More Fun with High *do*

"Buckeye Jim" is a folk song from the Appalachian region of the United States.

Sing the highlighted measures of "Buckeye Jim" using pitch syllables. What kind of scale does this song use?

CD 7:15

Appalachian Nonsense Song

Verse

1. Way up yon - der a - bove the sky, A
2. Way up yon - der a - bove the moon, A
3. Way down yon - der in a wood - en trough, An'
4. Way down yon - der on a hol - low log, A

blue - bird lived in a jay - bird's eye.
blue jay nests in a sil - ver spoon.
old wo-man died of the whoop - in' cough.
red bird danced with a green bull - frog.

Play these parts on mallet instruments while the class sings "Buckeye Jim."

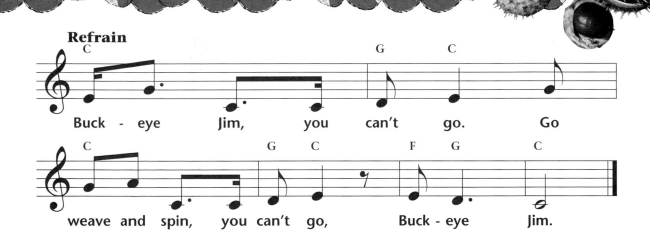

Refrain

Buck - eye Jim, you can't go. Go

weave and spin, you can't go, Buck - eye Jim.

Listening for ♪♩ ♪

The Inca and Quechua people are native to Bolivia and Peru. They have made flutes from wood, clay, or bone for centuries. Two of these types of flutes are called panpipes and the *quena*.

LISTENING CD 7:21

Festival Dance Peruvian folk melody

"Festival Dance" is a traditional tune from Peru played on panpipes and *quenas*.

Clap the rhythm pattern shown below. **Listen** for this rhythm in "Festival Dance."

How many times did you hear this rhythm played?

◁ A Quechuan man from Peru playing panpipes

An Incan man from Bolivia playing the *quena* ▽

Rhythm Scramble!

Read the patterns in the boxes below. **Listen** to the recording and identify the order the patterns are played.

Each of these patterns comes from music you have sung or heard. One is a mystery pattern. Match the pictures below with the rhythm patterns above and provide the title of the two pieces you know.

Glass Chords

Listen for the chord changes in "Dance No. 4."

 LISTENING CD 7:28

Dance No. 4 (excerpt) by Philip Glass

Listen to Philip Glass perform "Dance No. 4" on pipe organ.

Meet the Musician

Philip Glass (b. 1937) is an American composer and performer who first studied music in New York, and later in Paris. He has written music for ballet, musicals, opera, and movies. Glass continues to compose and explore new forms of music.

Learn About the Pipe Organ

The pipe organ is a keyboard instrument that dates back to the third century B.C. It has foot pedals and two or more sets of keys called manuals. The organ needs air to make sound. When playing the organ, air is forced through pipes of certain sizes. This creates the sound. A longer pipe will produce a lower sound. Shorter pipes produce higher sounds. Pipe organs can have hundreds and even thousands of pipes. The pipes are made of wood or metal.

Listen to "Dance No. 4" again as you follow the listening map. **Move** to identify the chord changes as you listen.

Listening Map for Dance No. 4

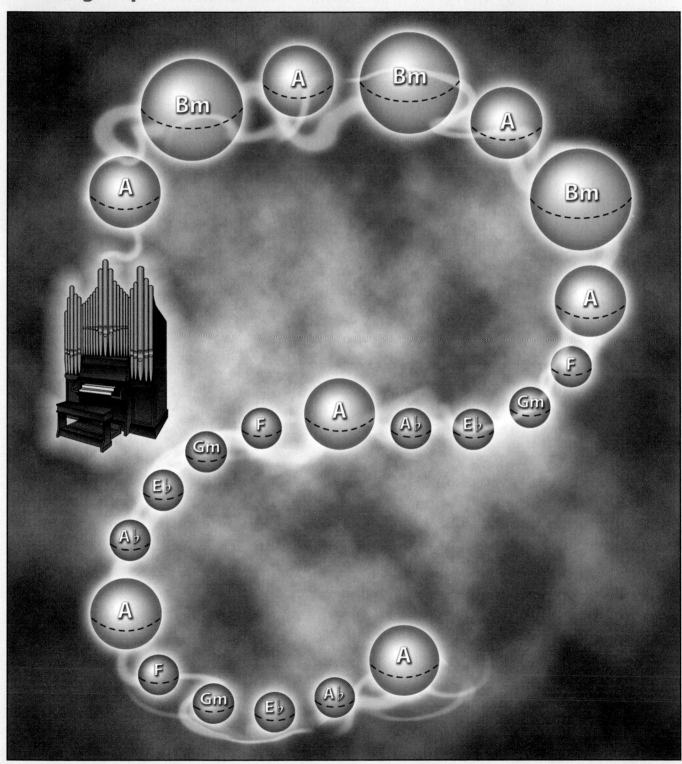

LESSON 6

Chords in Your Land

CONCEPT
HARMONY

SKILLS
SING, PLAY, IDENTIFY

LINKS
CULTURES, SOCIAL STUDIES

"This Land Is Your Land" describes the boundaries and beauty of the United States. **Sing** "This Land Is Your Land." What do you think is beautiful about this country?

This Land Is Your Land

CD 7:29

Words and Music by Woody Guthrie

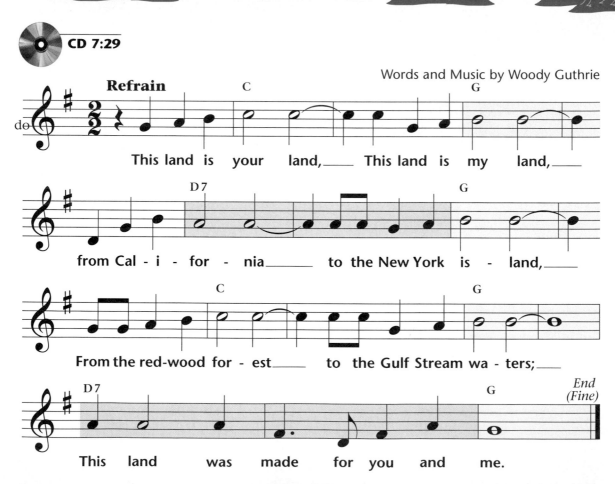

Refrain

This land is your land,___ This land is my land,___

from Cal - i - for - nia___ to the New York is - land,___

From the red-wood for - est___ to the Gulf Stream wa - ters;___

This land was made for you and me.

One Song, America, Before I Go (excerpt)

One song, America, before I go,
I'd sing, o'er all the rest, with trumpet sound,
For thee—the Future.

—*Walt Whitman*

Verse

1. As I was walk - ing____ that rib - bon of high - way,____
2. I've roamed and ram - bled____ and I fol-lowed my foot - steps____
3. When the sun comes shin - ing____ and I was stroll - ing____

I saw a - bove me____ that end - less sky - way.____
to the spar - kling sands of____ her dia - mond des - erts,____
and the wheat fields wav - ing____ and the dust clouds roll - ing____

I saw be - low me____ that gold - en val - ley,____
And all a - round me____ a voice was sound - ing,____
As the fog was lift - ing,____ a voice was chant - ing,____

Go back to the beginning and sing to the End.
(Da Capo al Fine)

This land was made for you and me.
"This land was made for you and me."
"This land was made for you and me."

Spotlight Your Success!

REVIEW

1 What is an octave?

  a. the five lines and four spaces on which musical notes are written

  b. the distance between two pitches that have the same name

  c. the stressed sounds that occur between the beats instead of on the beats of a rhythm pattern

  d. two or more pitches sung or played at the same time

2 What is a countermelody that is sung above the melody of a song?

  a. motive   **b.** round   **c.** descant

3 What is the root of this chord?

  a. A   **b.** D   **c.** G

READ AND LISTEN

1 **Read** these rhythms. Then listen. Which rhythm do you hear?

  a. [musical rhythm notation in 2/4 time]

  b. [musical rhythm notation in 2/4 time]

  c. [musical rhythm notation in 2/4 time]

  d. [musical rhythm notation in 2/4 time]

2 **Read** these patterns using pitch syllables. Then listen. Which pattern do you hear?

THINK!

1 How would you explain syncopation?

2 How could you determine if two notes were an octave apart?

3 What do the lyrics of "This Land Is Your Land " mean to you? Why?

4 **Write** about a concept you learned in this unit and tell why you think it is important.

CREATE AND PERFORM

1 Choose ♪ ♩ ♪, ♫, ♩, ♩, and 𝄽 to fill four measures in ⁴⁄₄ meter.

2 **Create** your own rhythm composition.

3 **Play** your composition using percussion instruments.

4 For an additional challenge, use pentatonic pitches in the key of F to create a melody for your composition.

Meet the Musician

ON NATIONAL RADIO!

Name: Lauren Criddle
Age: 15
Instrument: Voice
Hometown: Calabasas, California

When fifteen-year-old Lauren Criddle was in elementary school, the only kind of music she knew about was the pop music she heard on the radio. She wasn't exposed to classical music until she began studying voice.

When Lauren saw her first opera, she couldn't believe how magnificent it was. She said to herself, "This is me! This is what I want to do with the rest of my life!" Lauren hopes that one day she'll sing at famous opera houses all over the world. She would also like to teach because she wants to expose other kids to classical music.

Lauren recently visited an elementary school where she taught children about opera. "At first, some of them chuckled and covered their ears," recalls Lauren, "but soon they were asking me all sorts of questions." Afterward, Lauren was asked to sign many autographs!

 LISTENING CD 8:8–9

Summertime from *Porgy and Bess*
by George and Ira Gershwin

Listen to Lauren's performance and interview on the national radio program **From the Top**.

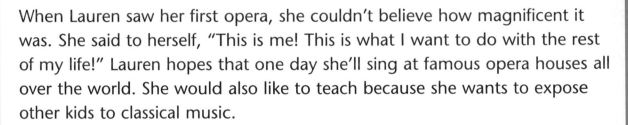

RECORDED INTERVIEW

Spotlight on the Violin

Did You Know?

Violinists produce sounds either by pulling a bow across the strings—*arco*—or by plucking the strings with their fingers—*pizzicato*.

Before the middle 1700s, violinists rested the instrument on their chests, not their shoulders.

The violin section is the largest group of instruments in the orchestra.

Antonio Stradivari (1644–1737) is considered the most gifted *luthier*, or violin maker, in history.

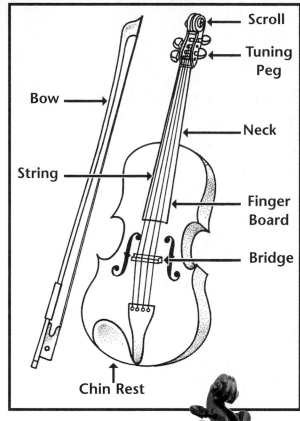

Scroll
Tuning Peg
Bow
Neck
String
Finger Board
Bridge
Chin Rest

 LISTENING CD 8:10–11

Scheherazade (excerpt)
by Nikolai Rimsky-Korsakov

Summer (Allegro on Molto) from *The Four Seasons* (Concerto No. 2 in G Minor) (excerpt)
by Antonio Vivaldi

Listen to the violin. In "Scheherazade" you can hear it play from a medium low register, where your own voice may reach, up to the very highest notes. In Vivaldi's *Summer*, the expressive qualities of the violin can be heard. Vivaldi was a violinist himself, and wrote many concertos for his favorite instrument.

One Musical Planet

People all over the world speak different languages and have different ways of life. Music is one thing they all share. In Unit 5 you will sing and listen to music that brings to life the rich heritage of many lands. What are some songs you know that come from other lands?

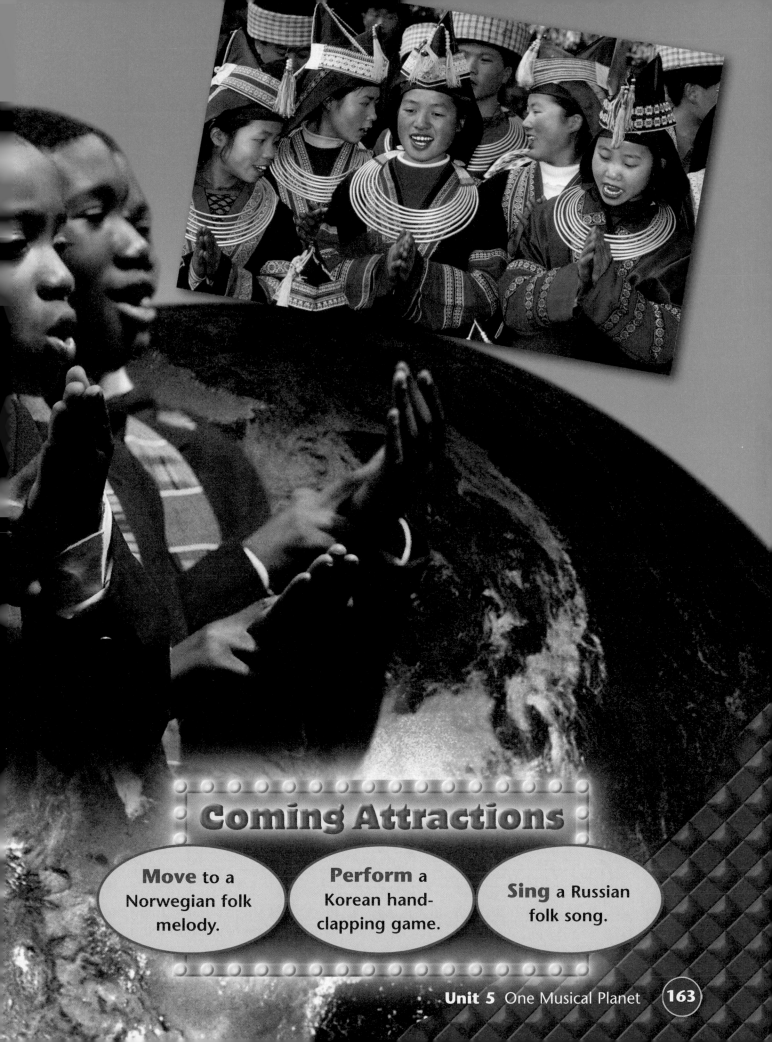

Coming Attractions

Move to a Norwegian folk melody.

Perform a Korean hand-clapping game.

Sing a Russian folk song.

Music has the power to unite all people on Earth.
What are some other things that unite us?

Sing "Just One Planet."

CD 8:12

Words and Music by
Sarah Stevens and Catherine Marchese

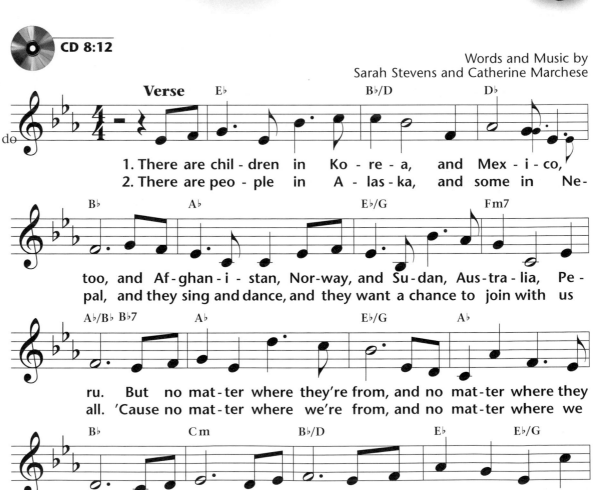

1. There are chil - dren in Ko - re - a, and Mex - i - co,
2. There are peo - ple in A - las - ka, and some in Ne-

too, and Af - ghan - i - stan, Nor - way, and Su - dan, Aus - tra - lia, Pe -
pal, and they sing and dance, and they want a chance to join with us

ru. But no mat - ter where they're from, and no mat - ter where they
all. 'Cause no mat - ter where we're from, and no mat - ter where we

go, they all live, they all love, and there's some - thing they should
go, we all live, we all love, and there's some - thing we should

CONCEPT
METER
SKILLS
SING, IDENTIFY, LISTEN, PERFORM
LINKS
CULTURES, VISUAL ARTS, MOVEMENT

When running, track athletes may need to run faster. Sometimes they just need to keep a steady pace. In music, this steady pace is the steady beat.

"Sansa kroma" is a game song played by children of the Akan culture in Ghana. **Sing** "Sansa kroma" and play the stone-passing game with the steady beat. **Identify** the meter of the song.

MAP
MALI   BURKINA FASO
IVORY COAST   GHANA   NIGERIA
TOGO   BENIN
WEST AFRICA

Sansa kroma

Little Hawk

 **CD 8:15**

Akan Game Song
English Words by Linda Worsley

Ashanti: San - sa⎯ kro - ma, Ne na wu‿o ɔ - kye-kyer nko - kɔ ma
Pronunciation: san sa kɾo ma ne na wuɔ ɔ che che n̥ko kɔ ma
English: San - sa⎯ kro - ma, Lit - tle hawk, You are an or-phan now.

San - sa⎯ kro - ma, Ne na wu‿o ɔ - kye-kyer nko - kɔ ma
san sa kɾo ma ne na wuɔ ɔ che che n̥ko kɔ ma
San - sa⎯ kro - ma, Lit - tle hawk, You are an or-phan now.

166

1. Grab

2. Pass

3. Clap

4. Clap

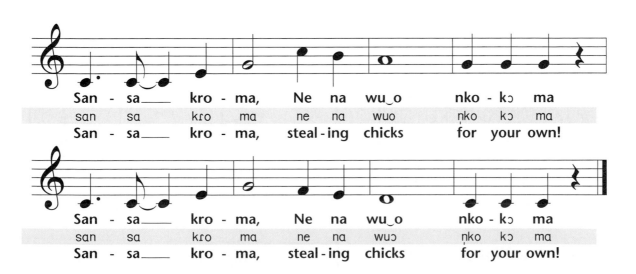

San - sa___ kro - ma, Ne na wu_o nko - kɔ ma
san sa kɾɔ ma ne na wuo nko kɔ ma
San - sa___ kro - ma, steal - ing chicks for your own!

San - sa___ kro - ma, Ne na wu_o nko - kɔ ma
san sa kɾɔ ma ne na wuɔ nko kɔ ma
San - sa___ kro - ma, steal - ing chicks for your own!

Dancing—Norwegian Style!

Listen to "Nokken Danser." **Pat** your legs when you feel the downbeat. **Tap** your shoulders on the other beats. Which meter signature fits best? $\frac{2}{4}$, $\frac{3}{4}$, or $\frac{4}{4}$?

 LISTENING CD 8:19

Nokken Danser Norwegian folk melody

"Nokken Danser" is a folk tune from Norway. The original melody has been around for hundreds of years.

Perform the dance for "Nokken Danser." Form a circle in pairs. Take one step for every downbeat.

Move counterclockwise in a circle.

Move clockwise in a circle.

Art Gallery

A Watermill in Christiania

This oil painting was created by Louis Gurlitt (1812–1897) around 1834. It shows a watermill in Norway.

B

Move into the circle and form a star.

Switch parts and move into the circle.

CONCEPT
TONALITY

SKILLS
SING, MOVE, LISTEN

LINKS
MOVEMENT, CULTURES, SOCIAL STUDIES

The word "Shalom" is Hebrew for "peace."
"Shabat Shalom" is a joyful wish for peace.
Sing the song.

MAP

ISRAEL
GAZA
WEST BANK
JORDAN
EGYPT
SAUDI ARABIA

Shabat Shalom

CD 8:20

Words and Music by N. Frankel

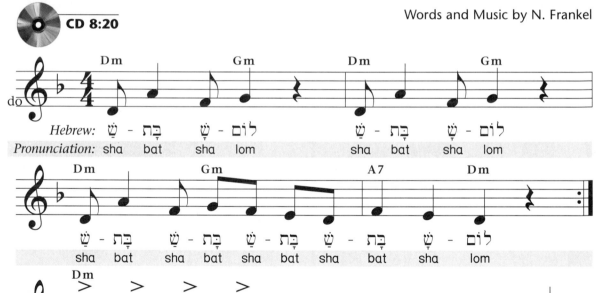

Hebrew: שַׁ - בָּת שָׁ - לוֹם   שַׁ - בָּת שָׁ - לוֹם
Pronunciation: sha bat sha lom   sha bat sha lom

שַׁ - בָּת שָׁ - בָּת שָׁ - בָּת שָׁ - בָּת שָׁ - לוֹם
sha bat sha bat sha bat sha bat sha lom

שַׁ - בָּת שָׁ - בָּת שָׁ - בָּת שָׁ - בָּת שָׁ - לוֹם
sha bat sha bat sha bat sha bat sha lom

שַׁ - בָּת שָׁ - בָּת שָׁ - בָּת שָׁ - בָּת שָׁ - לוֹם
sha bat sha bat sha bat sha bat sha lom

One reason melodies sound different from one another is that they use different sets of pitches. Some songs use a set of pitches called **major**. Others use a set of pitches called **minor**. The set of pitches used in "Shabat Shalom" is minor.

The grapevine step is often used in dances from the Middle East. **Perform** this step as you sing "Shabat Shalom."

RIGHT
Step right.

BACK
Cross your left foot behind your right and step.

RIGHT
Step right.

HOP
Hop with your right foot and kick with your left.

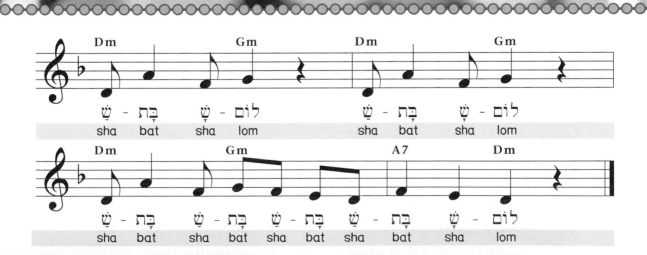

Major Nonsense!

"Chumbara" is a song that uses a set of pitches in major.
The words do not mean anything, but the song is fun to sing!
Sing "Chumbara."

MAP

CANADA
ALASKA
UNITED STATES

CD 8:24

Canadian College Song

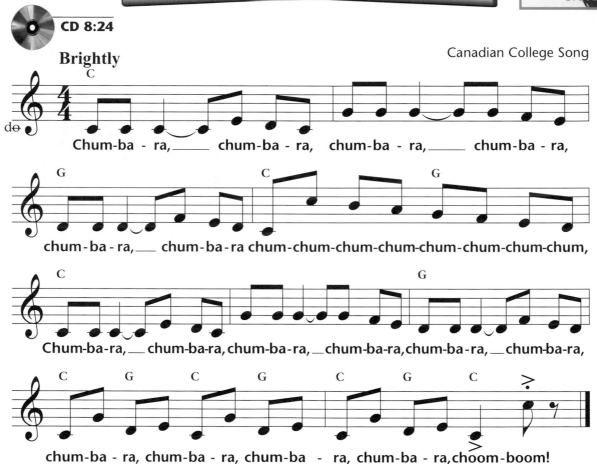

Brightly

Chum-ba - ra, ____ chum-ba - ra, chum-ba - ra, ____ chum-ba - ra,

chum-ba - ra, ___ chum-ba - ra chum-chum-chum-chum-chum-chum-chum-chum,

Chum-ba-ra, __ chum-ba-ra, chum-ba-ra, __ chum-ba-ra, chum-ba-ra, __ chum-ba-ra,

chum-ba - ra, chum-ba - ra, chum-ba - ra, chum-ba - ra, choom-boom!

THINK!

How do you think "Chumbara" would sound if it were minor? How would this change the mood of the song?

An Ear for Major and Minor

Listen to "Dance of the Mirletons" as you follow the listening map below.

 LISTENING CD 8:27

Dance of the Mirletons from *The Nutcracker*
by Piotr Ilyich Tchaikovsky

"Dance of the Mirletons" is from *The Nutcracker*, a ballet suite. A mirleton is a type of reed instrument. This selection has A and B sections that repeat. The A section is played by three flutes. A trumpet is featured in the B section. One section is in major, and one section is in minor.

Which section is major and which is minor?

Meet the Musician

Piotr Ilyich Tchaikovsky (1840–1893), a Russian composer, wrote ballets, operas, symphonies, concertos, and choral music. Many people said that he wrote his music from the heart, not the head.

Listening Map for Dance of the Mirletons

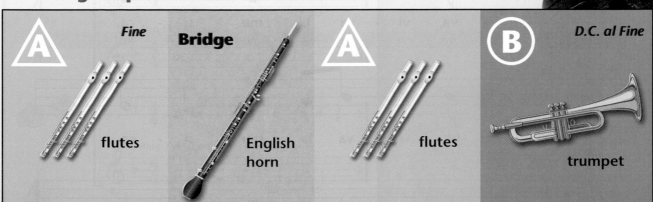

Renaissance Rhythms

Listen to "La canarie."

LISTENING CD 9:1

La canarie from *Dances from Terpsichore*
by Michael Praetorius

"La canarie" is an instrumental piece Michael Praetorius composed for dancing. It is taken from a larger work called *Dances from Terpsichore.* This recording features the bagpipe, a common instrument during Praetorius' time.

Look at the melody below from "La canarie." **Identify** the ♩. ♪ rhythm each time it occurs.

See **music.mmhschool.com** to research Renaissance Music.

▲ *Bagpipe Player* (bronze statue, 16th century) by Giambologna

Learn About Renaissance Music

Between 1400 and 1550, the sound of music changed very quickly. Musical forms and harmonies became more full and complex. Many of the new musical ideas were created by French and Flemish composers. With the help of the printing press, these ideas spread quickly through the churches and royal courts of Europe.

THE RAMAGE PRESS.

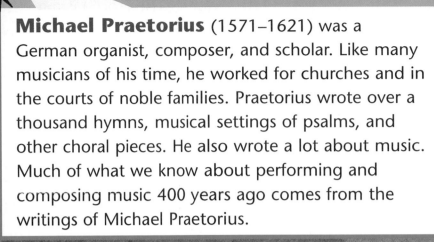

Michael Praetorius (1571–1621) was a German organist, composer, and scholar. Like many musicians of his time, he worked for churches and in the courts of noble families. Praetorius wrote over a thousand hymns, musical settings of psalms, and other choral pieces. He also wrote a lot about music. Much of what we know about performing and composing music 400 years ago comes from the writings of Michael Praetorius.

Art Gallery

Two Musicians

Albrecht Dürer (1471–1528) created this painting around 1504, about 70 years before Praetorius was born.

CONCEPT
MELODY
SKILLS
SING, IDENTIFY, READ
LINKS
CULTURES, SOCIAL STUDIES

"El coquí" ("The Frog") is a folk song from Puerto Rico. **Sing** the song with the Spanish words.

MAP
THE BAHAMAS
CUBA
JAMAICA
HAITI
DOMINICAN REPUBLIC
PUERTO RICO

El coquí

The Frog

CD 9:5

Puerto Rican Folk Song
English Version by MMH

Verse

Spanish: El co - quí, el co - quí a mi me en can - ta,
Pronunciation: el ko ki el ko kia mi men kan ta
English: The co - quí, the co - quí so en - tranc - ing,

Es tan lin - do el can - tar del co - quí;
es tan lin doel kan tar ðel ko ki
The co - quí sings a beau - ti - ful song.

Por las noch - es al ir a a - cost - ar - me,
por las no ches al ir a kos tar me
Through the hours when I'm sleep - ing and dream - ing,

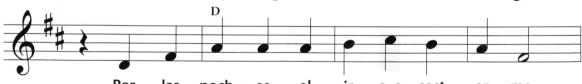

Me a - dor - me - ce can - tan - do a - sí.____
mea ðor me se kan tan do a si
The co - quí sings to me all night long.____

Almost "*do*" but Just Below

Sing the last phrase of "El coquí" shown below.
Then sing just the last pitch, the tonal center, *do*.
The highlighted pitch just below *do*ᴵ is called *ti*.
Identify *ti* in "El coquí."

ti

so   do ᴵ   do ᴵ   ti   la   ti   do ᴵ

Read this phrase using pitch syllables and hand signs.

Refrain

A   D   A7   D

Co - quí,   co - quí,   co - quí, quí, rí, quí.
ko   ki   ko   ki   ko   ki   ki   ri   ki

A   D   A7   D

Co - quí,   co - quí,   co - quí, quí, rí, quí.
ko   ki   ko   ki   ko   ki   ki   ri   ki

CONCEPT
METER
SKILLS
SING, MOVE,
LISTEN, PAT
LINKS
LANGUAGE
ARTS, CULTURES,
MOVEMENT

"**R**oll On, Columbia" is about the Columbia River in the northwestern United States. **Sing** the song. How might you move to show the meter?

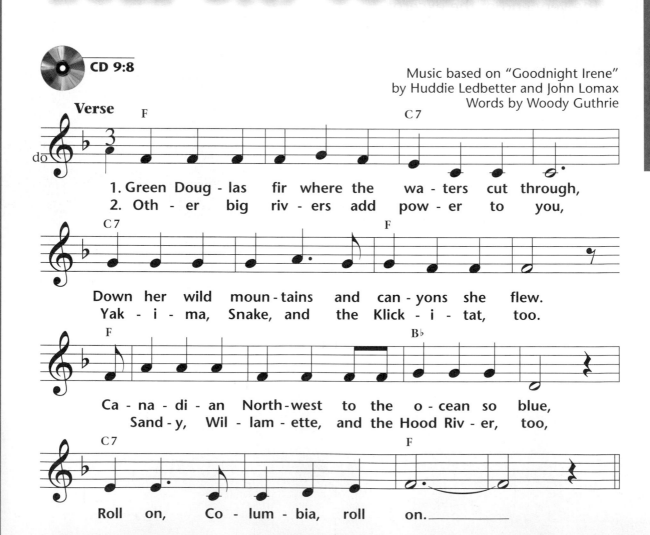

ROLL ON, COLUMBIA

CD 9:8

Music based on "Goodnight Irene"
by Huddie Ledbetter and John Lomax
Words by Woody Guthrie

Verse

1. Green Doug - las   fir where the   wa - ters   cut through,
2. Oth - er   big   riv - ers add   pow - er   to   you,

Down her   wild   moun - tains   and can - yons she   flew.
Yak - i - ma, Snake, and   the Klick - i - tat,   too.

Ca - na - di - an   North - west   to the   o - cean so   blue,
   Sand - y,   Wil - lam - ette,   and the Hood Riv - er,   too,

Roll   on,   Co - lum - bia,   roll   on._____

Corre el río
(The River Flows By)

Corre el río
decidido, sin parar
el mar sereno

The river flows by
Determined, instoppable
The ocean serene

—*Patricia Vasquez*

Columbia River

The meter signature of "Roll On, Columbia"
is $\frac{3}{4}$ meter. $\frac{3}{4}$ meter can also be written as $\frac{3}{4}$ meter.
How many beats are there per measure in $\frac{3}{4}$ meter?
Which note gets one beat?

Refrain

Roll on,____ Co-lum-bia, roll on. Roll on,____ Co-
lum-bia, roll on. Your pow-er is turn-ing our
dark-ness to dawn. Roll on, Co-lum-bia, roll on.____

A Hand-Clapping Game from Korea

"Ban Dal" is a song from Korea. There is a hand-clapping game that goes with the song. **Listen** to "Ban Dal." Learn to play the game.

MAP

RUSSIA

CHINA

NORTH KOREA

JAPAN

SOUTH KOREA

 LISTENING CD 9:11

Ban Dal by Yoon Kyekyoung

This song was written by the Korean composer Yoon Kyekyoung in the 1920s. It is known by many Korean children. Kyekyoung is considered to be a Korean national treasure by many native Koreans.

Pat with the beat as you listen to "Ban Dal" again. The beats are in groups of three.

Look at the Korean characters. Read the
translation as you listen to the song again.

반 달

Ban Dal
Half Moon

1 푸른 하늘 은하수 하얀 쪽배엔
계수 나무 한 나무 토끼 한 마리
돛대도 아니 달고 삿대도 없이
가기도 잘도 간다 서쪽 나라로

2 은하수를 건너서 구름나라로
구름나라 지나선 어디로 가나
멀리서 반짝반짝 비치이는 건
샛별이 등대란다 길을 찾아라

1 In the blue sky, the milky way and a white boat
In the boat, a laurel tree and a little rabbit
While having no mast or even a punt pole
It moves smoothly to western lands

2 Moving toward the other side of the milky way to the
    land of clouds
What will be encountered past cloud-land?
Sparkling in the far distance,
The morning star, like a light house, will guide the way.

Minor or Major?

"Katyusha" is a folk song from Russia. **Sing** "Katyusha" in Russian first and then in English.

CD 9:15

Russian Folk Song
English by John F. Loud

Verse

Dm ... A7

Russian: 1. Рас - цве - та - ли яб - ло - ни и гру - ши,
Pronunciation: ɾas tsvɛ ta li yab la nyi i gɾu shi
English: 1. Bloom - ing were the ap - ple and the pear trees,

A7 ... Dm

По - плы - ли ту - ма - ны над ре - кой.
pɔ pli li tu ma ni nad ɾɛ kɔɪ
Swirl - ing o'er the ri - ver was the mist.

Refrain

Dm B♭ F Gm Dm

Вы - хо - ди - ла на бе - рег Ка - тю - ша,
vi ha di la na bɛ ɾɛk ka tyu sha
All at once on the bank ap - peared Ka - tyu - sha,

Gm Dm Gm A7 Dm

На вы - со - кий бе - рег, на кру - той.
na vi sɔ ki bɛ ɾɛk na kɾu tɔɪ
On the high, the steep ri - ver bank.

188

Sing the first four measures using pitch syllables.

la₁ ti₁ do la₁ do do ti₁ la₁ ti₁ mi₁

Look at the last two measures of the song.
Name the pitch syllables and then sing them.

Listen to the song. **Identify** the key signature.
Is "Katyusha" in F major or D minor?
How do you know?

do
F major

la
D minor

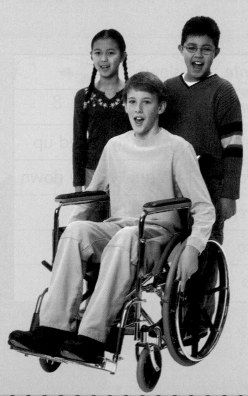

Tempo Changes for the Birds

This song tells a story about a different bird, "The Old Carrion Crow." **Listen** to the song. You will hear that the tempo of the verses is *allegro*, except for Verse 4.

Sing the song. Then choose the tempo for Verse 4 from this list.

accelerando	*ritardando*	*allegro*
presto	*moderato*	

MAP
GREENLAND
QUEBEC
NEW BRUNSWICK
NOVA SCOTIA

The Old Carrion Crow

CD 9:21

Nova Scotian Folk Song

Verse
mf

Dm   C   Dm   Am

do

1. Oh, the old car-rion crow was sit-ting on an oak,
2. Hur-ry now bring me my cross__ and my bow,
3. Oh, the tai - lor shot and missed_ his__ mark,
4. The__ old sow died and the bells__ did__ toll,
5. Oh,__ now the old sow's dead__ and__ gone,

Dm   C   Dm

Fol the rid-dle, all the rid-dle hey ding

(1.) doh,
(2.) doh,
(3.) doh, And he
(4.) doh, And the
(5.) doh, And the

192

THINK!

Read all the words to the song.
Why do you think the tempo is different in Verse 4?

Watch – ing a tai – lor cut - ting out a coat.
That I may shoot yon car - ri - on___ crow.
shot the mil - ler's sow right through_ the___ heart.
lit-tle pigs___ cried and prayed__ for her soul.
lit-tle pigs___ play and wad - dle___ on,

slightly held back

a tempo

Sing he, sing ho, the old car - rion crow, Fol the rid-dle, all the rid-dle

Refrain

slightly held back

hey ding doh. Ki - me - lea - ro kill my kea - ro, ki - me - lea - ro ki - mo,

a tempo

To me bump, bump, bump, jump Pol-ly wol-ly lee, Lin-ko kil-ly cum ki - mo.

CONCEPT
RHYTHM

SKILLS
SING, IDENTIFY, READ, CREATE

LINKS
CULTURES, SOCIAL STUDIES

"**L**as mañanitas" (The Morning Song) is a popular birthday song from Mexico. Children in Mexico hit a *piñata* while wearing a blindfold at birthday parties. A *piñata* is a decorated object filled with candy and toys.

Sing the song. **Identify** the ♩. ♪ in the song.

MAP
UNITED STATES
MEXICO   BELIZE
GUATEMALA

Las mañanitas
The Morning Song

CD 9:24

Mexican Folk Song
English Version by MMH

do

Spanish: Es	- tas	son	las	ma	- ña	- ni	- tas
Pronunciation: es	tas	son	las	ma	nya	ni	tas
English: Now	we	sing	*las*	*ma*	*- ña*	*- ni*	*- tas,*

que	can	- ta	- ba̮el	Rey	Da	- vid,
ke	kan	ta	ꞵael	ɾei	ða	ꞵið
as	King	Da	- vid	long	a	- go

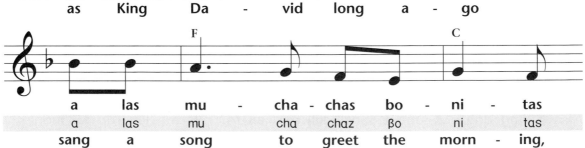

a	las	mu	- cha - chas	bo	- ni	- tas
a	las	mu	cha chaz	ꞵo	ni	tas
sang	a	song	to greet	the	morn	- ing,

se	las	can	- ta - mos	a	- sí:
se	las	kan	ta mos	a	si
to	greet	the	sun - light's	first	glow.

194

piñatas

THINK!

Read the song using pitch syllables.
Is this song in a major or minor key? How can you tell?

Des - pier - ta,	mi	bien,	des - pier - ta,
des pyeɾ ta	mi	βyen	des pyeɾ ta
A - wak - en,	dear	one,	a - wak - en

mi - ra	que	ya‿a - ma - ne - ció,
mi ɾa	ke ya	ma ne syo
and wel - come	the	ros - y dawn.

Ya	los	pa - ja - ri - tos	can - tan,
ya	los	pa xa ɾi tos	kan tan
Now	the	birds are sweet - ly	sing - ing,

la	lu - na	ya	se	me - tió.
la	lu na	ya	se	me tyo
the	sil - ver	moon - light	has	gone.

Unit 5 One Musical Planet

195

Play and Create Rhythms

Read these rhythms first using body percussion. Then play them with percussion instruments.

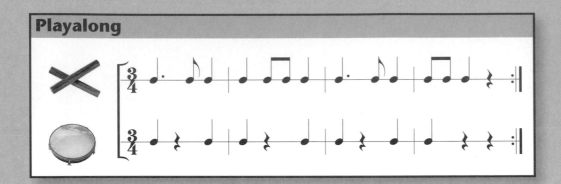

Playalong

Perform these rhythms as an accompaniment to "Las mañanitas."

Create Rhythm!

Create your own rhythm composition to fill eight measures in $\frac{3}{4}$ meter.

Use ♩. ♪ , ♩ , ♫ , and 𝄽 for your composition. Use ♩ 𝄽 𝄽 in the last measure of your composition. **Play** your rhythm on percussion instruments.

Listen to "Las mañanitas." How is this recording different from the song?

 LISTENING CD 9:28

Las mañanitas Mexican song

This recording features "Las mañanitas" played by the mariachi group Mariachi Vargas de Tecalitlán.

guitarra del golpe

Meet the Musicians

Mariachi Vargas de Tecalitlán is named for its founder, Gaspar Vargas. Founded in 1898, it has been one of the most popular mariachi groups in Mexico. The group started with only three members playing a violin, harp, and *guitarra del golpe* (a small five-string guitar). Over the years they have added more players and instruments.

Spotlight Your Success!

1 What is the Italian word for tempo that means to gradually speed up?

    a. *moderato*   **b.** *allegro*   **c.** *presto*   **d.** *accelerando*

2 What is the name of the scale for the eight pitches between *la,* and *la*?

    a. minor scale   **b.** pentatonic scale   **c.** major scale

3 What are the pitch syllables for this melody?

    a. *so fa | mi fa | so so re re | so fa so ||*

    b. *do' ti | do' ti | la la fa fa | mi re mi ||*

    c. *do' ti | la ti | do' do' so so | do' ti do' ||*

1 **Read** these rhythms. Then listen.
Which rhythm do you hear?

2 **Read** these patterns using pitch syllables. Then listen. Which pattern do you hear?

a.

b.

c.

THINK!

1 How would you change a song in duple meter to triple meter?

2 If you were to change a song in a major key to a song in a minor key, how would the sound be different?

3 If you were asked to compose a happy song, what tempo would you use? Why?

4 **Write** about two cultures you learned about in this unit. Compare language, rhythm, and instruments. Which music do you prefer? Why?

CREATE AND PERFORM

1 Choose ♩, ♩., ♪, ♩, ♫, and 𝄽 to fill eight measures in ¾ meter.

2 **Create** a melody by choosing pitches for your rhythm.

3 Use pitches from the major scale in the key of C or D. If you choose C, end your melody on C. If you choose D, end your melody on D.

4 **Sing** your melody using pitch syllables twice, once at a slower tempo, and once at a faster tempo.

Meet the Musician
ON NATIONAL RADIO!

Name: David Ross
Age: 15
Instrument: Flute
Hometown: North Mankato, Minnesota

Fifteen-year-old David Ross started playing piano at the age of seven, but it never felt quite right. He tried violin and clarinet, but they didn't seem to suit him either. Then one day he tried his sister's flute. He was surprised to find that playing it came very naturally to him. "I was immediately able to get a good sound," says David. "I figured I had a good start, so I kept on going."

Not only is David a flutist, he is also a weightlifter. "I first started lifting weights in ninth grade as part of gym class, and I really enjoyed it. I like pushing myself to the limit," he explains. These days, David can bench-press a whopping 215 pounds!

David enjoys all sorts of sports, but playing the flute is what he loves to do most of all. Next year he will attend a high school for the arts. He is looking forward to devoting more of his time to studying music.

 LISTENING CD 10:1–2

Sonata for Flute and Piano, Third Movement
by Francis Poulenc

Listen to David's performance and interview on the national radio program **From the Top.**

RECORDED INTERVIEW

Christopher Cerf learned early on how joyful music should be. When he was six years old, his uncle's friend taught him a little about notes and chords and how they worked together in songs. Mr. Cerf was hooked.

He was even more excited when he heard rock and roll artists like Fats Domino. It wasn't enough just to listen to the music, though. Mr. Cerf had to play it himself. By experimenting at the piano and using what he'd learned in lessons, Mr. Cerf began recognizing chord changes and musical patterns. He could play by ear and imitate many different musical styles. Soon he began writing his own songs.

Mr. Cerf's talent for writing scripts and his knowledge of children's media led him to *Sesame Street* at its beginning. Once there, he was asked to write music for the new show. It had to be fun and teach children, too. Mr. Cerf has been writing and singing for *Sesame Street* for 35 years now and is also Executive Producer, Music Producer, and Co-Creator of *Between the Lions*.

Mr. Cerf shares some advice with teachers and students. "Music is a joyful thing. Remember that while studying the hard parts."

Did You Know?

A trombonist plays different pitches by changing the length of the instrument's tubing. To change the length, the player slides a piece of the tubing in and out.

There are seven slide positions on a trombone.

A trombone's tubing is twice as long as a trumpet's.

 LISTENING CD 10:3–4

The Big Turtle—Fanfare from *The South China Sea*
by Gyorgy Ligeti

Pulcinella Suite (excerpt)
by Igor Stravinsky

Brass instruments were originally used for hunting calls and fanfares to announce important events. **Listen** to a solo trombone fanfare.

This song is about how one person can make a difference for a lot of people. The words talk about people who had dreams for a better future and worked to make those dreams come true.

Sing "What Can One Little Person Do?" What can you do to make a difference in other people's lives?

Rosa Parks ▲

◀ Harriet Tubman

What Can One Little Person Do?

CD 10:5

Words and Music by Sally Rogers

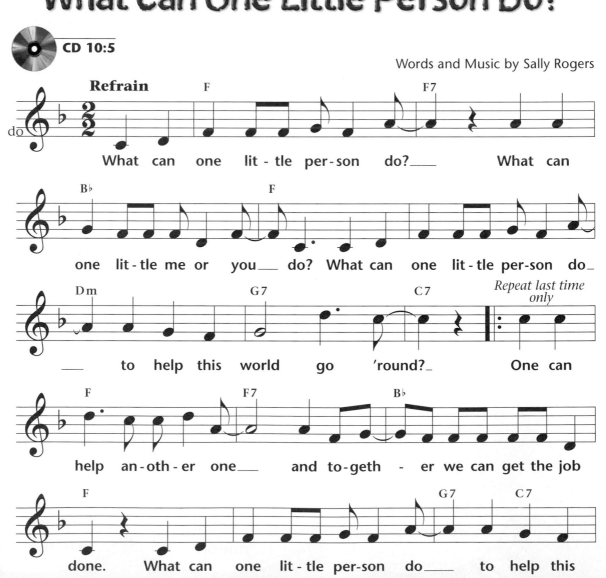

Refrain

What can one lit-tle per-son do?___ What can one lit-tle me or you___ do? What can one lit-tle per-son do___ to help this world go 'round?_ One can help an-oth-er one___ and to-geth - er we can get the job done. What can one lit-tle per-son do___ to help this

Repeat last time only

Martin Luther King, Jr. ▶

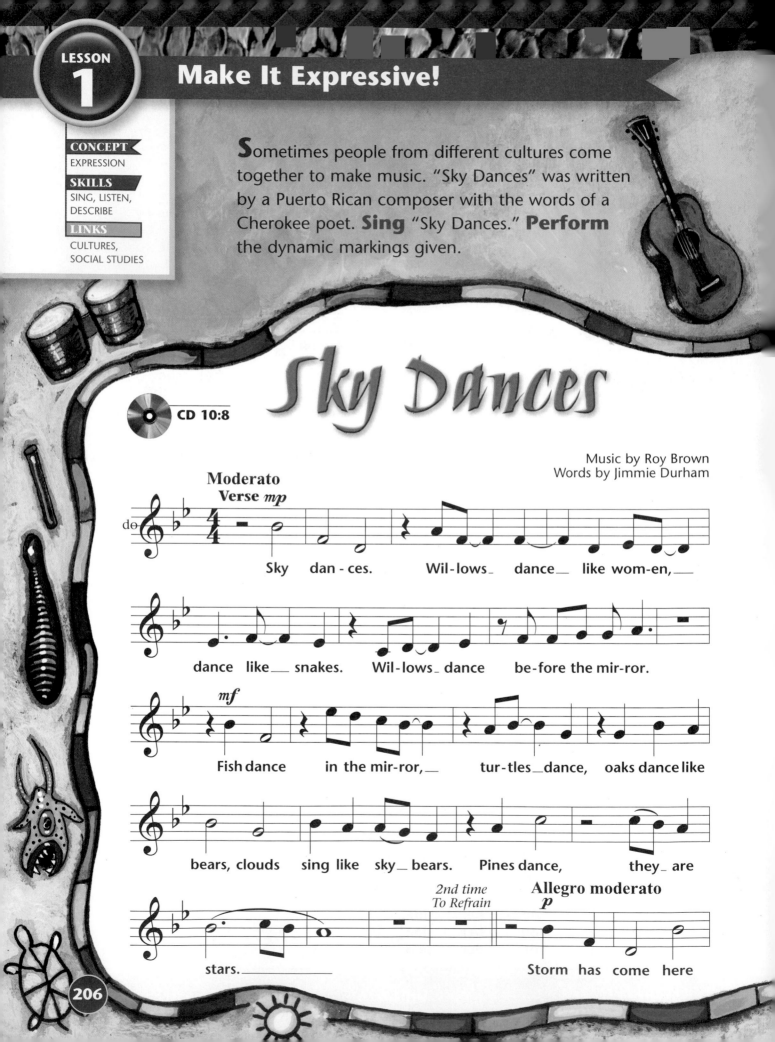

Learn About Fusion Music

Music that blends musical traditions of more than one culture is known as **fusion music**. This includes traditional songs performed in different styles. Fusion music can also be new compositions created by blending sounds, languages, and instruments of different cultures together.

Listen to these recordings. Think about how they are alike and how they are different. Use the terms below to describe how they are alike and different.

tempo	how fast or slow the music is
dynamics	how loud or soft the dynamics are
articulation	how the notes are played, such as short and crisp—**staccato**, or smooth and connected—**legato**

 LISTENING CD 10:11

Milan (Meeting of the Two Rivers) by Karsh Kale

This recording features folk and chamber music from India blended together with popular music from the United States and with unusual sounds.

 LISTENING CD 10:12

Porushka-Paranya Russian folk song

This recording features a folk song from Russia blended with American bluegrass, as performed by the group Bering Strait. **Name** some of the instruments you recognize from the jug band.

Listen for the different musical styles in each piece below. Can you tell what instruments are being used? **Describe** the tone colors you hear.

 LISTENING CD 10:14

Jangali Famata by Ali Farka Toure

This recording features traditional folk music from Mali in West Africa blended with blues music from the United States.

 LISTENING CD 10:13

Refavela by G. Gil

"Refavela" features rhythms and words from Benin in West Africa blended with Brazilian percussion. The message of this song is to take action and help people. What are ways you can help the other students in your school?

Meet the Musician

Angelique Kidjo (b. 1960) started performing at age 6 with her mother's theater troupe. Her music blends the styles of her West African, Brazilian, and English heritage. She toured Brazil with Ali Farka Toure. She views music as a common language shared by all people. Her songs are made up of conversations between instruments, percussion, and voices.

 Log on to **music.mmhschool.com** to learn more about fusion music.

Spinning Through History

CONCEPT
FORM
SKILLS
SING, LISTEN, DESCRIBE
LINKS
CULTURES, SOCIAL STUDIES

"**S**arasponda" came to the United States from the Netherlands. The nonsense words are used to imitate the sound of a spinning wheel. **Listen** for the two sections of the song. How are these sections different? **Sing** "Sarasponda."

Sarasponda

CD 10:16

Dutch Spinning Song

Sa - ra - spon-da, Sa - ra-spon-da, Sa - ra - spon-da, Ret - set - set!

Sa - ra - spon-da, Sa - ra - spon-da, Sa - ra - spon-da, Ret - set - set!

Ah - do - ray - oh! Ah - do - ray-boom-day - oh!

Ah - do - ray-boom-day, Ret - set - set! Ah - say - pa - say - oh!

Listening for Form

Listen to "Spinning Wheel" as you follow the listening map below.

 LISTENING CD 10:19

Spinning Wheel by David Clayton-Thomas

In this song the phrase *Ride a painted pony let the spinnin' wheel turn* tells you that the spinning wheel is a carousel. "Spinning Wheel" was a big hit in the late 1960s for the group Blood, Sweat & Tears. The group combined elements of jazz and rock and roll in their music.

Describe the ways in which Blood, Sweat & Tears made the sections different.

Listening Map for Spinning Wheel

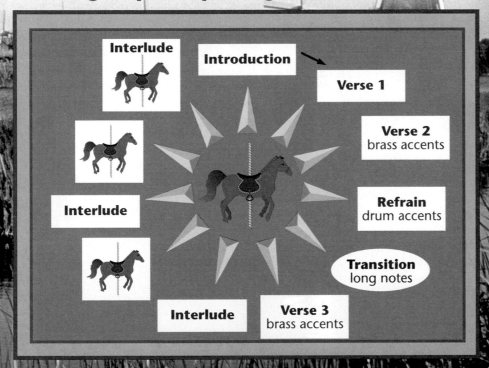

CONCEPT
RHYTHM

SKILLS
SING, COMPARE, READ

LINKS
MATH, VISUAL ARTS

"El barquito" ("The Tiny Boat") is a folk song from Panama. **Sing** the song in both Spanish and English.

MAP

NICARAGUA

COSTA RICA

PANAMA

COLOMBIA

El barquito

The Tiny Boat

CD 11:1

Panamanian Folk Song
English Version by MMH

Spanish: Ha - bía u - na vez un bar - co chi - qui - ti - to,_____
Pronunciation: a βyu na βes um baɾ ko chi ki ti to
English: Oh, once I had a pret - ty lit - tle sail - boat!____

ha - bía u - na vez un bar - co chi - qui - ti - to,_____
a βyu na βes um baɾ ko chi ki ti to
Oh, once I had a pret - ty lit - tle sail - boat!____

ha - bía u - na vez un bar - co chi - qui - ti - to,_____
a βyu na βes um baɾ ko chi ki ti to
Oh, once I had a pret - ty lit - tle sail - boat!____

Que no po - dí - a, que no po - dí - a,
ke no po ði a ke no po ði a
A - las, it could not, a - las, it could not,

214

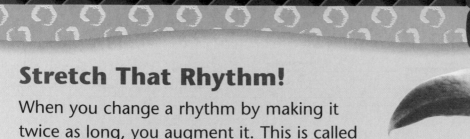

Stretch That Rhythm!

When you change a rhythm by making it twice as long, you augment it. This is called **augmentation**. When you augment a sound that is one beat long, it becomes a sound that is two beats long. If you were to augment a ♩ in 𝄴, it would become a ♩

Compare the patterns below. **Identify** the connection between the two patterns.

Here is another example of augmentation.

How would you augment this rhythm?

THINK!

Why do you think a composer would choose to use augmentation?

Art Gallery

Nevoa (Mist)

This oil painting was created by Bob Nugent (b. 1948). It shows the mist above the Amazon River in Brazil.

216

"Mighty River" is a fun speech piece that uses rhythms you know. **Read** the speech piece.

MIGHTY RIVER

Poem by Will Brecht
Adapted by MMH

CD 11:5

4/4

Deep in the land of the jun - gle green,

Where the li - on roars and the par - rots scream,

A might - y ri - ver from a ti - ny stream,

Lis - ten to it rush in - to the sea.

Now perform "Mighty River" in augmentation. Make each rhythm, or each word, twice as long. Keep the same beat as you perform the speech piece in augmentation.

Perform "Mighty River" in two groups. One group can perform the piece as written while the other group performs the piece in augmentation.

Unit 6 A Time to Dream, A Time to Sing

217

CONCEPT
HARMONY
SKILLS
SING, PLAY, COMPARE
LINKS
SOCIAL STUDIES, CULTURES

Singing two or more melodic lines together is one way to make harmony. This is called **polyphony**. Rounds, canons, descants, and countermelodies are types of polyphony. When harmony parts have the same words and rhythm as the melody, it is called **homophony**. **Sing** homophonic voice parts in the refrain of "Bamboo."

BAMBOO

CD 11:8

Words and Music by Dave Van Ronk

1. You take a stick of bam-boo, You take a stick of bam-boo, You
(2.) trav - el on the riv - er, You trav - el on the riv - er, You
(3.) home's a-cross the riv - er, My home's a-cross the riv - er, My

take a stick of bam-boo, You throw it in the wa-ter,
trav - el on the riv - er, You trav - el on the wa-ter, Oh____
home's a-cross the riv - er, My home's a-cross the wa-ter,

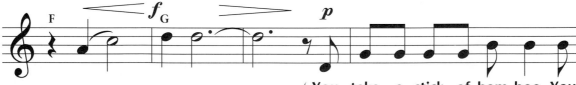

Oh____ Han - nah!____

You take a stick of bam-boo, You
You trav - el on the riv - er, You
My home's a-cross the riv - er, My

take a stick of bam-boo, You take a stick of bam-boo, You
trav - el on the riv - er, You trav - el on the riv - er, You
home's a - cross the riv - er, My home's a - cross the riv - er, My

Play these parts on mallet instruments while the class sings the song.

throw it in the wa-ter,
trav-el on the wa-ter,   Oh___   Oh___   Han-nah!___
home's a-cross the wa-ter,

Refrain

Riv - er,___   She come down.___

Riv - er,___   She come down.___

{ 2. You
{ 3. My

down.___   You take a stick of bam-boo, You take a stick of bam-boo, You

take a stick of bam-boo, You throw it in the wa-ter.___

Decorating with Sound

CONCEPT
MELODY
SKILLS
SING, LISTEN
LINKS
VISUAL ART, CULTURES

Many cultures take pleasure in decorating everyday items. Furniture, tools, musical instruments, and even plates are decorated. Designs are carved, sewn, etched, or painted onto objects to make them beautiful and special.

"Hala lala layya" is a folk song from Lebanon in the Middle East. **Sing** the song.

Art Gallery

Turkish table
This table is made from wood inlaid with ebony and ivory. It dates from the 1560s Ottoman Empire in Turkey.

Hala lala layya

CD 11:16

MAP
MEDITERRANEAN SEA
LEBANON
SYRIA
JORDAN
ISRAEL
EGYPT

Lebanese Folk Song
English lyrics by John Higgins

Pronunciation: ha la la la lei ya ha la la la lei ya

ai ni ya mu lei ya ta bil ha wa

English: **You are tru-ly____ dear_ to__me.** **To me our friend-ship_**

Melodies, like visual objects, can also be decorated. Extra pitches, or groups of pitches, added to melodies are called **ornaments**. In some musical styles, ornaments are added to a melody at will by the performer.

Look for the ornaments in "Hala lala layya." The ornaments add motion by filling in skips and moving by steps around pitches. **Identify** the ornaments in the song.

See **music.mmhschool.com** to research Middle Eastern music.

_____ ya hɩ lu ɑ max lɛɪ ɪsh wa _____ ya

_____ al-ways will_ be some-thing that I trea - sure.

2   *End (Fine)*   *Sing 1st time only*

læ' sʊ daɪ bu ɛl wə lɪf

wəs æl ɑ la dɑ ɾu   **To me our friend - ship_**

Go back to the beginning and sing to the End.
(D.C. al Fine)

_____ al-ways will_ be some-thing that I trea - sure.

223

Ornamentation—Dutch Style!

Ornamentation has been used for hundreds of years in music from many cultures. Jacob Van Eyck composed "Al Hebben de Princen haren" in the early seventeenth century. The piece begins with a simple melody in quarter notes. Below is the first phrase of the melody.

The melody is repeated two times. Each time it is decorated with more and more ornaments.

Listen for ornamentation in "Al Hebben de Princen haren."

🔵 **LISTENING** CD 11:20

Al Hebben de Princen haren by Jacob Van Eyck

This piece was written in the early seventeenth century. It is taken from a large collection of hundreds of pieces for recorder.

Meet the Musician

Jacob Van Eyck (c. 1589–1657) was born a nobleman in The Netherlands. He was blind from birth. Van Eyck was a composer, a scientist, and a designer of church bells. He was also the greatest recorder player of his time. He composed and collected hundreds of pieces for the recorder.

A carillon, used for ► playing church bells

CONCEPT
TONALITY
SKILLS
SING, LISTEN, COMPOSE
LINKS
CULTURES, SOCIAL STUDIES

"A la nanita nana" is a lullaby from Spain. This song is about a mother singing to her baby.

Sing "A la nanita nana."

MAP
FRANCE
PORTUGAL
SPAIN
MOROCCO   ALGERIA

A la nanita nana

A Little Lullaby

CD 11:28

Puerto Rican Carol
Arranged by Michael Braz
English Words by Linda Worsley

A Refrain

Spanish: A la na-ni-ta na-na, na-ni-ta na-na, na-ni-ta e - a.
Pronunciation: a la na ni ta na na na ni ta na na na ni ta e a
English: A la na-ni-ta na-na, na-ni-ta na-na, na-ni-ta e - a.

Mi ni-ño tie-ne sue - ño ben-di-to, se - a ben-di-to se - a.
mi ni nyo tye ne swe nyo ßen di to se a ßen di to se a
My sleep-y lit-tle ba-by, dream in bless-ed slum-ber, in bless-ed slum-ber.

B Verse

Tor-to-li-ta que can-tas en-tre la fron - da,
tor to li ta ke kan tas en tre la fron da
Lit-tle doves in the tree-top, Joy-ful-ly sing-ing,

fuen-te ci-lla que co-rres ru - mo-ro - sa.
fwen te si ya ke ko res ru mo ro sa
Lit-tle foun-tain__ leap-ing, splash-ing and mur-mur-ing.

230

Identify the change from major to minor in "A la nanita nana." What is the form of the song? Which section is in minor ? Which section is in major ?

The refrain of "A la nanita nana" is made of pitches from the D minor scale.

The sound is minor . What is the tonal center of the scale?

The verse of the song is made up of pitches from the D major scale.

The sound is major . What is the tonal center of the scale?

CONCEPT
FORM

SKILLS
SING, LISTEN,
ANALYZE

LINKS
LANGUAGE ARTS,
CULTURES,
MOVEMENT

This song is about following your dream no matter what happens. What are some of your dreams? **Sing** "Follow Your Dream." **Identify** the form.

Follow Your Dream

CD 12:5

Words and Music by Mary Donnelly
Arranged by George L.O. Strid

1. Ev - 'ry - bod - y needs a star to wish on___ when
2. It's the dream with - in your heart that keeps you go - ing,___ when

things you want seem far, far a - way._____ But
noth - ing in the world seems___ right._____ But

you must al - ways strive to keep your dream a - live, 'cause
hold on to your dreams how - ev - er things may seem. That

what you long for, can be yours some - day. }
shin - ing star will guide you through the night. }

Listen to "Theme and Variations."

Theme and Variations (excerpt)
by Wolfgang Amadeus Mozart

This piece is from "Serenade in B♭ Major" for 13 wind instruments. It was written in the 1780s. Listen for the wind instruments you know in the recording.

Dream Dust
Gather out of star-dust
        Earth-dust,
        Cloud-dust,
        Storm-dust,
And splinters of hail,
One handful of dream-dust
        Not for sale.

—Langston Hughes

B **Refrain**

If you fol - low your dream,_ tho' the road seems lone - ly.
       fol - low your dream,_ tho' you're tired of try - ing.

Fol - low your dream_ no mat - ter how far._____
Fol - low your dream,_ what - ev - er you do._____

Give it your best,_ you'll find suc - cess,_ if you
There'll come a time_ when you will find_ you can

1. just keep your eye_ on that star!_ If you

2. make all your dreams_ and your wish - es come true.

Making It Different

Sometimes music can be more interesting by keeping some things the same while other things change, or vary.

Vary the refrain of "Follow Your Dream." Keep the melody, or **theme**, of the refrain the same. Each time you sing it, change it in two or three of these ways to create a **variation**:

- Change the dynamics. Sing it louder, then softer. Change the dynamic level as you sing.

- Change the articulation. Sing it staccato (short and clipped), then legato (smooth and flowing).

- Change the accompaniment. Choose a percussion instrument. Add the instrument on the words *Follow your dream.*

Sing the song again. Repeat your variations as you sing. This time, add ornamentation to the melody of the refrain. Fill in skips and add steps as you sing the refrain for the last time.

 **THINK!** How is the meaning of the words changed by the way you sing the refrain?

Very Moving!

Listen to "Debka Kurdit."

 LISTENING CD 12:9

Debka Kurdit Yemeni Folk Dance

"Debka Kurdit" is a circle dance that is danced throughout the Middle East. The basic movement pattern presented in Part I is varied each time you repeat it. In the variations of the basic step, you step in and out in different ways.

Practice the steps below. **Dance** the "Debka Kurdit"!

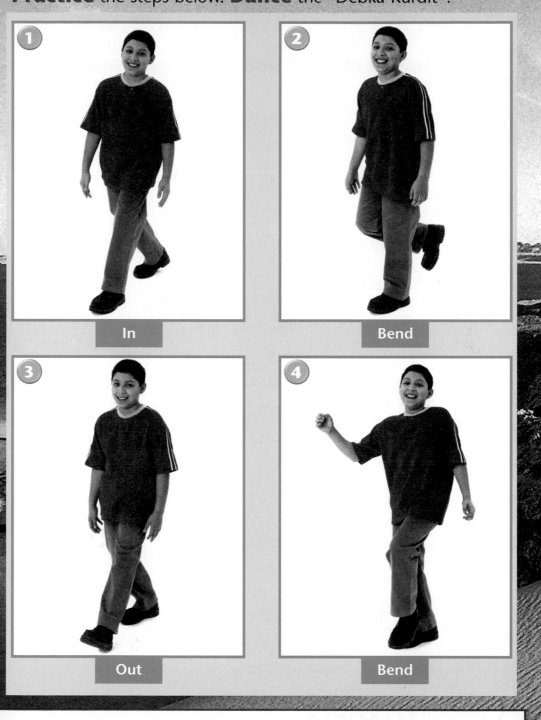

1. In
2. Bend
3. Out
4. Bend

Part 1 *4 times*

in   bend   out   bend

Part 2 *4 times*

in   hop   out   hop

Part 3 *4 times*

bounce, bounce, bounce, step

Part 4 *4 times*

in   hold   out, out, out

Part 5 *4 times*

in   bend   out   bend

Part 6 *4 times*

cross   side   cross   side

Spotlight Your Success!

REVIEW

1 What kind of music blends musical traditions of more than one culture?

    a. salsa   **b.** calypso   **c.** fusion   **d.** folk

2 What do you do when you augment a rhythm?

    a. change a rhythm by making it twice as short

    b. change the meter signature

    c. change a rhythm by making it twice as long

3 Which set of pitch syllables matches this melody?

    a. *so fa | mi re | do re mi fa | so mi do ‖*

    b. *do mi | so do' | ti la so fa | mi re do ‖*

    c. *do so, | do re | mi fa so fa | mi re do ‖*

READ AND LISTEN

1 **Read** these rhythms. Then listen. Which rhythm do you hear?

2 **Read** these patterns using pitch syllables.
Then listen. Which pattern do you hear?

THINK!

1 Describe what ornaments are and what they are used for.

2 What are some ways to vary a theme?

3 Tell in your own words the meaning of the lyrics of "What Can One Little Person Do?"

4 **Write** about the different styles of music you learned about in this unit. How would you describe the music using musical terms?

CREATE AND PERFORM

1 Choose ♩, ♫, ♩♫, ♫♫, and ♩ to fill four measures in ¾ meter.

2 **Create** a melody by choosing pitches for your rhythm.

3 Use pentatonic pitches in the key of F or G, where *la* is the tonal center.

4 If you choose F, end your melody on D. If you choose G, end your melody on E.

5 **Sing** your melody using pitch syllables. Use two or more dynamics as you sing.

Spotlight on
Music Reading

Spotlight on Music Reading

Practice Basic Rhythms

Rhythms are created with combinations of notes and rests.

A quarter note ♩ = one sound to a beat.
Two eighth notes ♫ = two sounds to a beat.
A quarter rest 𝄽 = one beat of silence.
A half note ♩ = a sound lasting two beats.

Read and practice these rhythms:

Ludwig van Beethoven

Read and play this ostinato.

🎵 **LISTENING** CD 12:10

Symphony No. 7 in A Major, Second Movement (excerpt) by Ludwig van Beethoven

This symphony uses the same rhythm pattern as the ostinato above.

Listen for the rhythm pattern in this selection.

CONCEPT ◄
MELODY

SKILLS
READ, SING

Sing with *Do, Re, Mi*

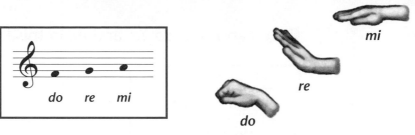

do   re   mi

Read and sing the repeated notes, steps, and skips in this song.

CD 12:11

Game Chant

do

1.-5. Did you ev-er, ev-er, ev-er in your
{ long - leg-ged
short - leg-ged
knock - kneed‿
bow - leg-ged
cross - leg-ged } life

Meet a long-leg-ged* sail-or with a long-leg-ged* wife?

No, I nev-er, nev-er, nev-er in my
{ long - leg-ged
short - leg-ged
knock - kneed‿
bow - leg-ged
cross - leg-ged } life

Met a long-leg-ged* sail-or with a long-leg-ged* wife.

Change word for verses 2.-5.

More *Do-Re-Mi* Melodies

Read and sing *do*, *re*, and *mi* in this Italian folk song.

do   re   mi

MAP

SWITZERLAND
FRANCE   ITALY   ALBANIA   GREECE

Farfallina

CD 12:15

Butterfly

Italian Folk Song
English Version by MMH

Italian: **Far-fal - li - na tut - ta bian - ca vo - la, vo - la, non si stan-ca.**
Pronunciation: far fal li na tut ta byang ka vo la vo la non si stang ka
English: **Far-fal - li - na, with your white wings, fly a-way, do not sit still.**

Vo - la li, vo - la la, po - si po - sa so-pra un fiore
vo la li vo la la po si po sa so praun fyore
Fly - ing here, fly - ing there, on a flow - er rest a while.

LISTENING CD 12:14

Carillon from *L'Arlesienne, Suite No. 1*
by Georges Bizet

Bizet wrote "Carillon" for a play called *L'Arlesienne (The Girl from Arles).*

Read and play this melody as you listen to "Carillon."

mi do re   mi do re   mi do re   mi

Improvise *do-re-mi* melodies in $\frac{3}{?}$ time as you listen again.

CONCEPT
MELODY
SKILLS
READ, SING

Sing with So

do re mi so

so

Read these songs with pitch syllables and hand signs.

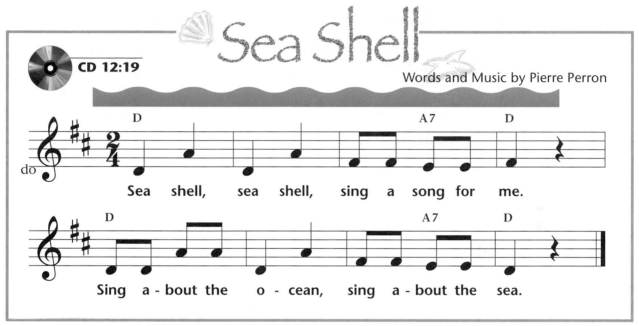

Sea Shell

CD 12:19

Words and Music by Pierre Perron

do

Sea shell, sea shell, sing a song for me.

Sing a - bout the o - cean, sing a - bout the sea.

Old Aunt Dinah

CD 12:22

African American Folk Song
Words Adapted by Ivy Rawlins

do

Old Aunt Di - nah, fare - well, fare - well, Old Aunt Di - nah,

fare thee well! Gone a - way to leave you, fare - well, fare - well,

Gone a - way to leave you, fare thee well!

Sing a Pentatonic Song

do re mi so la

la

la
so
mi
re
do

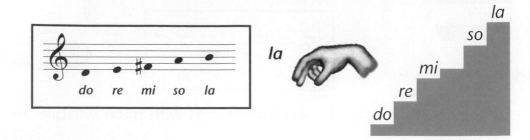

mi so so   la so so   la so mi mi do do   mi re do do

Identify the lowest and highest notes in this song.

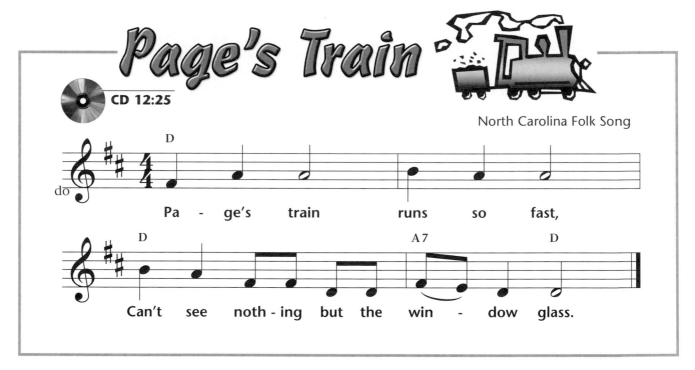

Page's Train

CD 12:25

North Carolina Folk Song

Pa - ge's train   runs   so   fast,

Can't   see   noth-ing   but   the   win - dow   glass.

Trains at Night
I like the whistle of trains at night,
The fast trains thundering by so proud!
They rush and rumble across the world,
They ring wild bells and they toot so loud!
But I love better the slower trains.
They take their time through the world instead,
And whistle softly and stop to tuck
Each sleepy blinking town in bed!   —*Frances M. Frost*

Sing and Create Pentatonic Melodies

Read this pentatonic song with hand signs.

Sing it with the words.

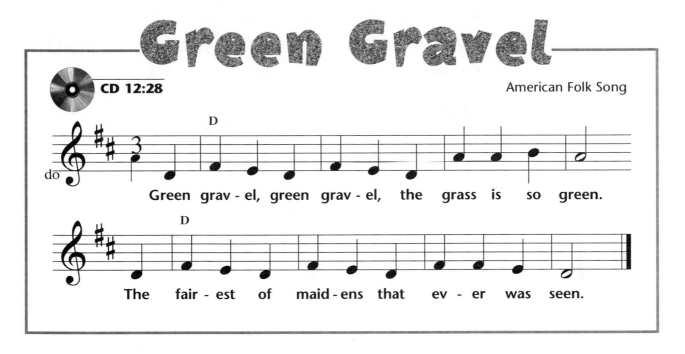

Green Gravel

CD 12:28

American Folk Song

do

Green grav - el, green grav - el, the grass is so green.

The fair - est of maid - ens that ev - er was seen.

Create a pentatonic melody using *do, re, mi, so,* and *la.*
Play it as a B section for "Green Gravel."

Sing with Low *So* and Low *La*

so₁ la₁ do re mi so la

Sing and play a game with this song that has low *so* and low *la*.

Hold My Mule

CD 12:31

Traditional Play Party Song

G   C   D7

1. Hold my mule while I dance, Jo-sey, Hold my mule while I dance, Jo-sey,

G   C   D7   G

Hold my mule while I dance, Jo-sey. O Miss Su-san Brown.

2. Wouldn't give a nickel if I couldn't dance, Josey, . . .
O Miss Susan Brown

3. Had a glass of buttermilk, then danced, Josey, . . .
O Miss Susan Brown

Sing this ostinato, first with pitch syllables then with the words.

Hold my mule, hold my mule, hold my mule, hold my mule.

Read and clap the rhythm of the song as you sing it. What do you notice about the rhythms in the second and third verses?

Sixteenth Notes

Four equal sounds to a beat can be written as four sixteenth notes (♫♫).

♫♫ = ♫ = ♩

The Girl I Left Behind Me

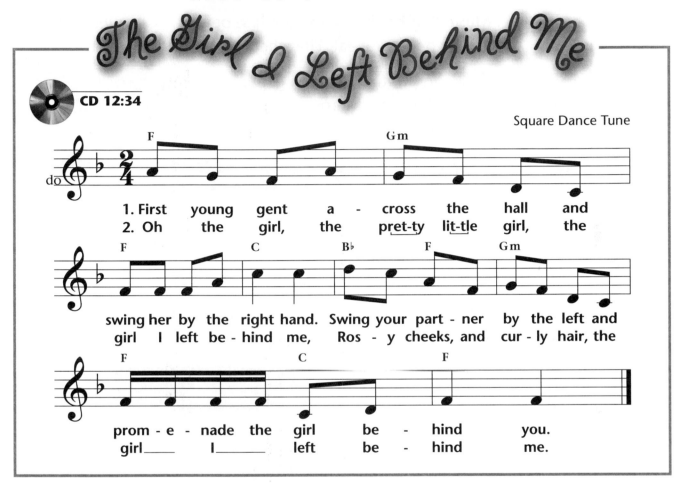

CD 12:34

Square Dance Tune

1. First young gent a - cross the hall and swing her by the right hand. Swing your part - ner by the left and prom - e - nade the girl be - hind you.

2. Oh the girl, the pret-ty lit-tle girl, and the girl I left be - hind me, Ros - y cheeks, and cur - ly hair, the girl____ I____ left be - hind me.

Improvise a rhythm ostinato for this song.

Sing this part of the song with pitch syllables and letter names.

F   F   F   F   C   D   F   F
do do do do so₁ la₁ do do

A *do* tonal center means the melody of a song is centered around *do*. The tonal center is often the last note of a song. What is the tonal center of this song?

Music Reading   249

Perform Sixteenth Notes

Three unequal sounds to a beat can be written with two sixteenth notes and one eighth note (♪ ♫ or ♫♪).

Remember, ♪ ♫ = ♩ and ♫♪ = ♩

Music that begins before the first beat of a complete measure begins on an upbeat. Find the upbeat.

Say and pat this Mexican game with sixteenth-note patterns.

MAP
UNITED STATES
MEXICO
BELIZE
GUATEMALA

Molinillo de café

Little Coffee Mill

CD 13:1

Latin American Children's Game
English Version by MMH

Spanish: Mue - le el mo - li - ni - llo de ca - fé.
Pronunciation: mwe lel mo li ni yo ðe kɑ fe
English: Lit - tle cof - fee mill gives us a treat,

Mue - le los gra - ni - tos pa - ra us - ted.
mwe le los gra ni tos pa rɑus teð
Grind - ing lit - tle cof - fee beans to - day.

Gi - ra con la ma - no, gi - ra con el pie,
hi ra kon la ma no hi ra kon el pye
Turn it with your hands and turn it with your feet,

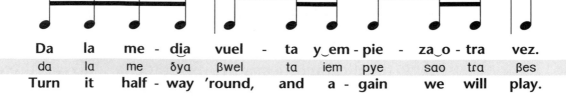

Da la me - dia vuel - ta y em - pie - za o - tra vez.
da la me ðya ßwel ta iem pye sɑo tra ßes
Turn it half - way 'round, and a - gain we will play.

A Different Tonal Center

Some songs have a pitch other than *do* or *la* as the tonal center. **Read** this pattern and identify the tonal center.

so, so, la, la, do re | do do la, la, do

do mi do do la, la, | do do la, la, so,

Ridin' of a Goat, Leadin' of a Sheep

CD 13:5

North Carolina Folk Song

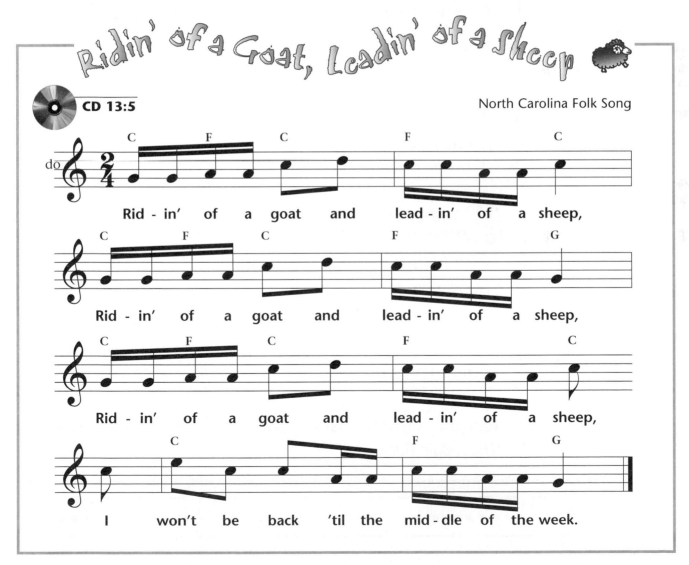

Rid - in' of a goat and lead - in' of a sheep,

Rid - in' of a goat and lead - in' of a sheep,

Rid - in' of a goat and lead - in' of a sheep,

I won't be back 'til the mid - dle of the week.

Music Reading **251**

Create with Sixteenth Notes

Remember, an eighth rest ♧ = a silence for half a beat and ♫ = ♩

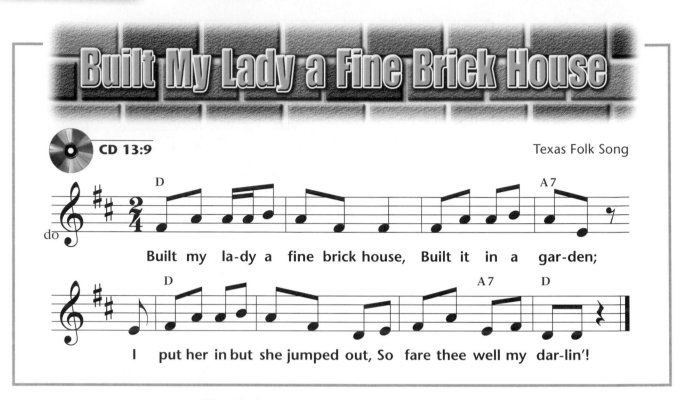

CD 13:9   Texas Folk Song

Built my la-dy a fine brick house, Built it in a gar-den;

I put her in but she jumped out, So fare thee well my dar-lin'!

LISTENING CD 13:8

The Magic Flute (Overture)
by Wolfgang Amadeus Mozart

The Magic Flute is an opera that combines both serious and comical ideas and music. The overture reveals these two contrasting characteristics.

Read this rhythm pattern and listen for it in the Overture to *The Magic Flute.*

Sing Sixteenth Notes

Find the measure with [♪♪♪] and the measure with [♪♪]

Swapping Song

CD 13:12 **Verse**

Appalachian Folk Song

1. When I was a lit-tle boy I lived by my-self;___
2. Rats___ and the mice,___ they___ led me such a life, I
3. Roads___ were so long___ and the lanes were so nar-row, I
4. Wheel-bar-row broke___ and my wife got a fall;___
5. Swapped my wheel-bar-row and___ got me a horse;___

All the bread and cheese I had, I put it on the shelf.___
had to go to Lon-don to___ get my-self a wife.___
had to bring her home___ in an old___ wheel-bar-row.
Down___ came the wheel-bar-row, wife___ and___ all.___
Then___ I___ rode___ from___ cross___ to___ cross.___

Refrain

Wing wong wad-dle, to my jack straw strad-dle, To my

John-nie fair fad-dle, to my long ways home.

6. Swapped my horse and got me a mare;
   Then I rode from fair to fair.

7. Swapped my mare and got me a mule;
   Then I rode like a doggone fool.

8. Swapped my mule and got me a goat;
   When I got on him, he wouldn't tote.

9. Swapped my goat and got me a sheep;
   Then I rode myself to sleep.

10. Swapped my sheep and got me a cow;
    And in that trade I just learned how.

Listen for Sixteenth Notes

LISTENING CD 13:15

"Galop" from *The Comedians* by Dmitri Kabalevsky

A galop is a type of fast, springy dance popular in nineteenth-century Europe. It is thought to have originated in Hungary. This music describes traveling comedians.

Look at the listening map. Find the A section rhythm, the Interlude rhythm, and the B section rhythm. Practice tapping each one at a quick tempo.

Listen to "Galop" and follow the listening map.

Listening Map for "Galop"

Use What You Know

Clap the rhythm of the first line.
What is the tonal center?

MAP
MEDITERRANEAN SEA
LEBANON
SYRIA
JORDAN
ISRAEL
EGYPT

Zum gali gali

CD 13:16

Israeli Work Song

Ostinato

Em   Am   Em

Hebrew: זום גָ-לִי, גָ-לִי, גָ-לִי, זום גָ-לִי, גָ-לִי,

Pronunciation: zum ga li ga li ga li zum ga li ga li

English: Zum ga-li, ga-li, ga-li, Zum ga-li, ga-li.

Verse

Em   Am   Em

הֶ-חָ-לוּץ לְ-מַעַן עֲ-בוֹ-דָה,

hɛ xa lutz lɛ ma'an a vo da

Pi-o-neers work hard on the land,

Em   Am   Em

עֲ-בוֹ-דָה לְ-מַעַן הֶ-חָ-לוּץ.

a vo da lɛ ma'an hɛ xa lutz

Men and wom-en work hand in hand.

Em   Am   Em

עֲ-בוֹ-דָה לְ-מַעַן הֶ-חָ-לוּצ,

a vo da lɛ ma'an hɛ xa lutz

As they la-bor all day___ long,___

Em   Am   Em

הֶ-חָ-לוּץ לְ-מַעַן עֲ-בוֹ-דָה.

hɛ xa lutz lɛ ma'an a vo la

They___ lift their voi-ces in song.

Music Reading 255

A Game in $\frac{6}{8}$ ($\frac{2}{\text{♩.}}$) METER

In $\frac{2}{\text{♩.}}$ meter, a dotted quarter note ♩. = one beat.

At slower tempos, an eighth note ♪ = one beat. The meter is then shown as $\frac{6}{8}$.

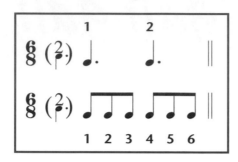

Read and pat the rhythms in the slower $\frac{6}{8}$ meter and the faster $\frac{2}{\text{♩.}}$ meter.

Perform the speech piece.

CD 13:20

Tea Leaves

Mexican Children's Game
English Version by MMH

$\frac{6}{8}$

Spanish: Ho - jas de té, ho - jas de té.
Pronunciation: o xɑs ðe te o xɑs ðe te
English: Here leaves of tea, There leaves of tea.

Ho - jas y ho - jas y na - da de té.
o xɑs i o xɑs i nɑ ðɑ ðe te
Tea leaves and tea leaves, but no cups of tea.

Perform the traditional Mexican hand patterns for this speech piece.

Sing Unequal Rhythms

Read and clap these rhythms.

Describe what is different about these rhythmic patterns.

Listen for unequal sounds to the beat as you learn to sing this song.

Goodbye, My Riley O

CD 13:24

African American Song
from the Georgia Sea Islands
Collected and Adapted by Lydia A. Parrish

1. Ri - ley,   Ri - ley, where are you?
2. Ri - ley gone to   Liv - er - pool.
3. Ri - ley gone to   Lon - don Town.
4. Ri - ley gone to   Mo - bile Bay.
O   Ri - ley   O   man!

Ri - ley gone and   I goin' too, Good - bye my Ri - ley   O!

A Sea Chantey in $\frac{6}{8}$

A tie ⌣ is a curved line that connects two notes of the same pitch and means that the sound is held for the length of the two notes.

In $\frac{6}{8}$ meter,  and

A dotted half note ♩ sounds for the whole measure.

Clap these rhythm patterns in $\frac{6}{8}$ meter.

Find these patterns in the song then sing it.

Heave-Ho, Me Laddies

CD 13:27

Sea Chantey

Oh, if I were a sail-or out a sail-ing on the sea,____
I real-ly am quite cer-tain____ a cap-tain I would be.
Heave-ho, me lad-dies. Fast-en down the sails.____
This blust'-ry wind will take us____ a-sail-ing o'er the sea. sea.

Practice ⁶⁄₈ Rhythms

Read and sing another ⁶⁄₈ song with ties.

The Derby Ram

CD 13:30

English Folk Song
Ozark Version

Verse F

do

1. As I went down to Der - by town all
2. The wool up - on this ram's___ back it
3. The horns up - on this ram's___ head they
4. The ears up - on this ram's___ head they
5. Oh ev - 'ry tooth this ram___ had would

F   C7   F

on a sum - mer's day,___ It's there I saw the
drug___ to the ground,___ I hauled it to the
reached_ to the moon,___ The butch-er went up on
reached_ to the sky,___ The ea - gle built his
hold a bush-el of corn,___ And ev - 'ry foot he

B♭   C7   F

fin - est ram that's ev - er fed on hay.___
mar - ket and it weighed ten thou - sand pounds.___
Feb - ru - ar-y and nev-er got back 'til June.___
nest there for I heard the young ones cry.___
stood___ on would cov-er an a-cre of ground.___

Refrain F   C7

And if you don't be - lieve me,___ and think I tell a lie,___

F   B♭   C7   F

Just you go down to Der - by and you'll see the same as I.___

Sing with *Fa*

so₁ do re mi fa so la

fa

Sing the orange patterns in this song
with pitch syllables.

MAP

SWITZERLAND
FRANCE
ITALY
SPAIN

Frère Jacques

Are You Sleeping?

CD 14:1

French Folk Song
Traditional English Words

1
F

do

French: **Frè - re   Jac - ques,   Frè - re   Jac - ques,**
Pronunciation: fɾɛ   ɾə   ʒɑ   kə   fɾɛ   ɾə   ʒɑ   kə
English: **Are   you   sleep - ing,   are   you   sleep - ing,**

2
F

Dor - mez - vous,   dor - mez - vous?
dɔɾ   me   vu   dɔɾ   me   vu
Broth - er   John,   Broth - er   John?

3
F

Son - nez   les   ma - ti - nes,   son - nez   les   ma - ti - nes,
sɔ   ne   le   mɑ   ti   nə   sɔ   ne   le   mɑ   ti   nə
Morn - ing   bells   are   ring - ing,   morn - ing   bells   are   ring - ing,

4
F

Din,   dan,   don,   din,   dan,   don.
dɛ̃   dɑ̃   dɔ̃   dɛ̃   dɑ̃   dɔ̃
Ding,   ding,   dong,   ding,   ding,   dong.

More Practice with *Fa*

Find *fa* in this American song.

Who's Got a Fishpole?

CD 14:5

American Folk Song

Group 1   Group 2   Group 1   Group 2

F   C7

1. Who's got a fish-pole? We do. Who's got a fish-pole? We do.
2. Who's got a line?__ We do. Who's got a line?__ We do.
3. Who's got a hook?_ We do. Who's got a hook?_ We do.

Group 1   Group 2   Group 1

F   C7   F

Who's got a fish-pole? We do.   Fish-pole needs a line.
Who's got a line?__ We do.   Line__ needs a hook.
Who's got a hook?_ We do.   Hook_ needs a worm.

Read the rhythm of this melody by Bach then sing it with pitch syllables.

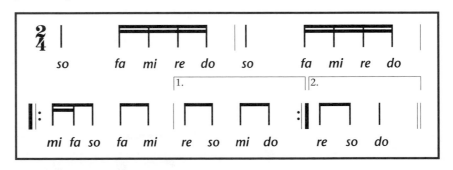

so   fa   mi   re   do   so   fa   mi   re   do

mi fa so   fa   mi   re   so   mi   do   re   so   do

 LISTENING   CD 14:8

Musette from *Notebook for Anna Magdalena Bach* by Johann Sebastian Bach

Listen to "Musette" and raise your hand when you hear the melody you just sang. Play the melody on a pitched instrument.

Use What You Know

Read and sing this pattern.

do   do   la   so   fa   mi   re   do

A slur ‿ is a curved symbol that tells you to sing a syllable on more than one pitch.

Find the slur in this song.

What is the meter?

Identify the rhythms you know.

Sing the song with pitch syllables and hand signs then with the words.

It Rained a Mist

CD 14:9   Virginia Folk Song

It rained a mist, it rained a mist.

It rained all o - ver the town, town, town.

It rained____ all o - ver the town.

Sing this theme from a symphony by Haydn with pitch syllables.

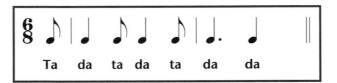
LISTENING CD 14:12

"La Chasse" ("The Hunt") *Symphony No. 73, Fourth Movement* by Franz Joseph Haydn.

Haydn wrote more symphonies than any other composer—108 in all. At the beginning of "La Chasse" ("The Hunt"), the pitches *do, mi,* and *so* suggest a hunting horn call. You will hear this theme throughout the movement.

The French horn of Haydn's time didn't have valves like horns today. That means they were not able to play all of the notes modern French horns play. Horn players had to change instruments to change keys, or insert longer or shorter "crooks" or tubing in order to play a variety of notes.

Listen for the theme played by the French horns.

Say or tap this rhythm ostinato as you listen again.

How does the music suggest galloping horses?

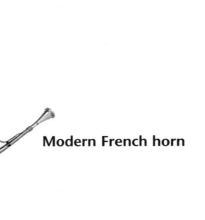

Modern French horn

CONCEPT
RHYTHM
SKILLS
IDENTIFY, PLAY, SING

Practice Syncopation

You know that ♩ = ♫

You can write a syncopated pattern like this: ♫♩♫ or like this: ♪ ♩ ♪

Identify the syncopated patterns in this spiritual.

How Long the Train Been Gone?

CD 14:13

African American Spiritual

1. How long the train been gone?_____
2. Train_____ been gone a long time.
3. Wave down the gos - pel train._____
4. Hand me my walk - ing cane._____
5. You'd bet - ter fall in line._____

How long the train been gone?
Train_____ been gone a long time.
Wave down the gos - pel train.
Hand me my walk - ing cane.
You'd bet - ter fall in line.

How long the train been gone?_____
Train_____ been gone a long time.
Wave down the gos - pel train._____
Hand me my walk - ing cane._____
You'd bet - ter fall in line._____

O yes, Lord.

Syncopation in Song

This song begins on beat two.

Sing the syncopated patterns in this song.

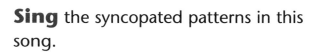

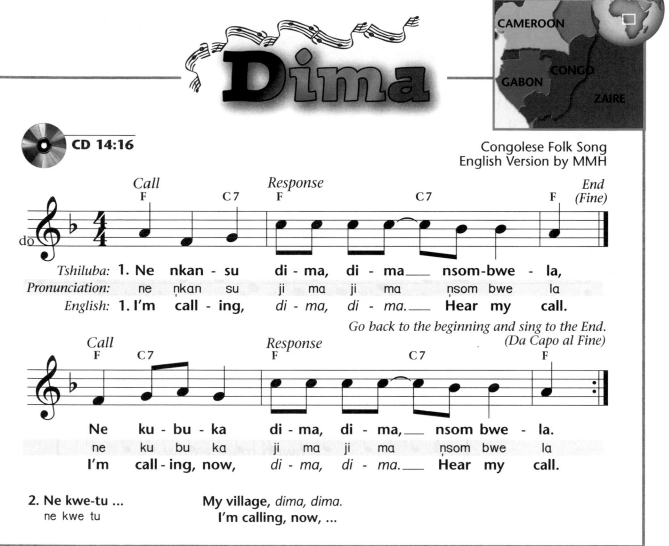

CD 14:16

Congolese Folk Song
English Version by MMH

MAP

CAMEROON

GABON   CONGO

ZAIRE

Call
F   C 7   Response
F   C 7   F   End (Fine)

Tshiluba: **1.** Ne nkan - su di - ma, di - ma___ nsom-bwe - la,
Pronunciation: ne nkan su ji ma ji ma nsom bwe la
English: **1.** I'm call - ing, *di - ma,* *di - ma.*___ **Hear** my call.

Go back to the beginning and sing to the End.
(Da Capo al Fine)

Call
F   C 7   Response
F   C 7   F

Ne ku - bu - ka di - ma, di - ma,___ nsom bwe - la.
ne ku bu ka ji ma ji ma nsom bwe la
I'm call - ing, now, *di - ma,* *di - ma.*___ **Hear** my call.

2. Ne kwe-tu ...   My village, *dima, dima.*
ne kwe tu   I'm calling, now, ...

Play these patterns as you sing the song.

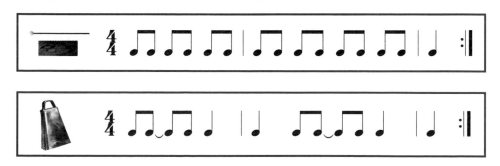

A Pentatonic Spiritual

Read and sing the response parts of this pentatonic song.

Read the pink part with pitch syllables then sing the song.

Train Is A-Coming

CD 15:1

African American Spiritual

Call   E♭   *Response*   A♭   E♭

1. Train is a - com - ing,   Oh,   yes,_____
2. Bet-ter get your tick - et,   Oh,   yes,_____
3. Room for man - y oth - ers,   Oh,   yes,_____

Call   E♭   *Response*   B♭

Train is a - com - ing,____ Oh,   yes,_____
Bet-ter get your tick - et,____ Oh,   yes,_____
Room for man - y oth - ers,____ Oh,   yes,_____

E♭   Cm

Train is a - com - ing,   Train is a - com - ing,
Bet-ter get your tick - et,   Bet-ter get your tick - et,
Room for man - y oth - ers,   Room for man - y oth - ers,

E♭   A♭   E♭

Train is a - com - ing,   Oh,   yes._____
Bet-ter get your tick - et,   Oh,   yes._____
Room for man - y oth - ers,   Oh,   yes._____

Practice Pitches and Rhythms

Sing this Shaker song with high *do.*

Find the largest leap in the melody. What is this leap called?

CD 15:4

Shaker Song

Hop Up and Jump Up

1
C
do

Hop   up and jump   up and   whirl 'round, whirl 'round,

C

Gath - er   love,   here   it   is   all   'round,   all   'round,

C

Here   is   love   flow - ing 'round,   catch   it   as   you whirl 'round,

C

Reach   up   and reach   down,   here   it   is   all   'round.

Identify high *do* each time it occurs with a hand sign.

What word would you use to describe the rhythm of the first bar?

Say or play this ostinato with the song.

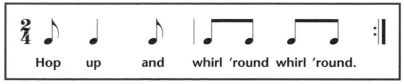

2
4

Hop   up   and   whirl 'round whirl 'round.

Another Dotted Rhythm Pattern

A dotted quarter note is equal in length to one quarter note plus an eighth note.

Clap these rhythm patterns.

Read the ♩. ♪ pattern in this song as you pat with the beat.

Chairs to Mend

CD15:7

Old English Round

Chairs to mend, Old chairs to mend!

Mack - er - el, Fresh mack - er - el! An - y

old rags, An - y old rags?

Sing the song in canon.

Practice with Rhythm Patterns

This song has another kind of rhythm pattern that uses a dotted quarter note: ♪ ♩.

Read the song and find the syncopated rhythms.

Clap these rhythm patterns, and identify those that appear in the song.

Create a body percussion ostinato using the patterns above.

CONCEPT
RHYTHM

SKILLS
SING, LISTEN, READ

American Cowboy Songs in ¾

Sing and conduct these cowboy songs in ¾ meter with ♩. ♪ rhythm patterns.

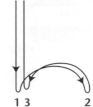

1 3   2

My Home's in Montana

CD 15:14

Cowboy Song

1. My home's in Mon - tan - a, I wear a ban - dan - na,
2. When val - leys are dust - y, My po - ny is trust - y,
3. When far from the ranch - es, I chop the pine branch - es,

My spurs are of sil - ver, My po - ny is gray.
He lopes through the bliz - zard, The snow in his ears.
To heap on my camp - fire As day - light grows pale.

When rid - ing the rang - es, My luck nev - er chang - es,
The cat - tle may scat - ter, But what does it mat - ter?
When I have par - tak - en Of beans and of ba - con,

With foot in the stir - rup I'll gal - lop a - way.
My rope is a hal - ter for pig - head - ed steers.
I whis - tle a mer - ry old song of the trail.

LISTENING CD 15:17

Cattle from *The Plow That Broke the Plains*
by Virgil Thomson

Listen for "My Home's in Montana" in this selection.

274

Read this song and identify the dotted half notes.

American Folk Song
Arranged by Mary Goetze

CD 15:18

Good - bye, Old Paint, I'm a - leav - in' Chey - enne.

Ride! Ride! Gid - dy up! Gid - dy up!

Good - bye, Old Paint, I'm a - leav - in' Chey - enne.

Ride! Ride! Gid - dy up! Gid - dy up!

I'm a - leav - in' Chey - enne, And I'm off to Mon - tan'.

Leav - in' Chey - enne. Off to Mon - tan'.

Good - bye, Old Paint, I'm a - leav - in' Chey - enne!

Ride! Ride! Gid - dy up! Gid - dy up!

Accompany a Song with Chords

Identify the pitch from the major scale that is missing in the song.

CABALLITO BLANCO
Little White Pony

CD 15:30

Mexican Folk Song
English Version by MMH

Spanish: 1. Ca - ba - lli - to blan - co, sá - ca - me de a quí.___
Pronunciation: ka βa yi to βlang ko sa ka me ðea ki
English: 1. Ca - ba - lli - to blan - co, Take me far a - way,___

Llé - va - me a mi pue - blo don - de yo na - cí.
ye βa mea mi pwe βlo ðon de yo na si
Take me to my birth - place, Where I want to stay.

2. Tengo, tengo, tengo,
tú no tienes nada.
Tengo tres borregas
en una manada.

tenggo tenggo tenggo
tu no tyenes naða
tenggo tres βoīegas
en una manaða

There will I have plenty,
Though you may be poor.
My three goats are tethered
By my cottage door.

3. Una me da leche,
otra me da lana
otra mantequilla
para la semana.

una me ða leche
otra me ða lana
otra mantekiya
para la semana

One will give me milk,
One his wool to wear.
One will give me butter,
We'll be happy there!

Play these chords to accompany the song.

G so   D⎮ re⎮
E mi   B ti
C do   G so

Find the letter-name markings for these chords in the song. In which measures do the chords change?

CONCEPT ► MELODY
SKILLS ► READ, SING, CREATE

Create with the Major Scale

The *bodeen* and the *carakeen* are types of traditional Irish boats.

Read this song to practice all the pitches in a major scale.

MAP
SCOTLAND
ATLANTIC OCEAN
NORTHERN IRELAND
ENGLAND
WALES
IRELAND

Oro, My Bodeen

CD 15:34

Irish Folk Song

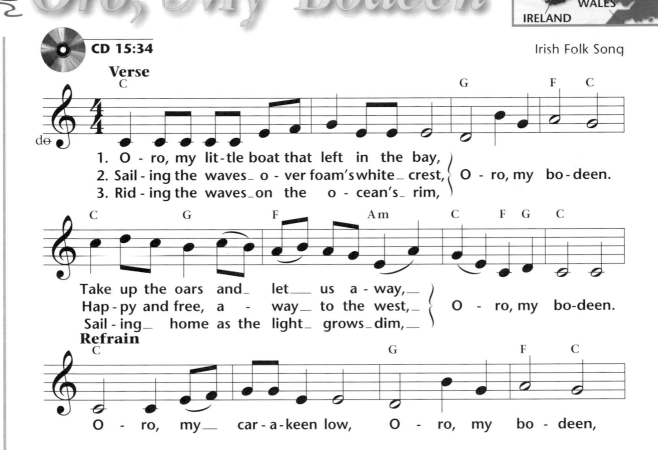

Verse

1. O - ro, my lit-tle boat that left in the bay,
2. Sail - ing the waves o - ver foam's white crest,
3. Rid - ing the waves on the o - cean's rim,

O - ro, my bo-deen.

Take up the oars and let us a - way,
Hap - py and free, a - way to the west,
Sail - ing home as the light grows dim,

O - ro, my bo-deen.

Refrain

O - ro, my car - a-keen low, O - ro, my bo - deen,

O - ro, my car-a-keen low, O - ro, my bo - deen.

Create a melody with words about sailing. Use the rhythm pattern from the first line of "Oro, My Bodeen." Use the pitches in a major scale, including *ti.*

A Song with a Different Tonal Center

Sing this song with pitch syllables and identify the tonal center.

CD 16:9

African American Work Song

Call | *Response* | *Call*
Old house, Tear it down! Who's gon-na help me

Response | *Call* | *Response*
Tear it down? Bring me a ham-mer, Tear it down!

Call | *Response* | *Call*
Bring me a saw,___ Tear it down! Next thing you bring me,

Response | *Call* | *Response*
Tear it down! Is a wrecking ma-chine, Tear it down!

Find the syncopated rhythms in the song.

An accent (>) in music puts more emphasis on a note.

Read this ostinato. Play it with the song on unpitched instruments of your choice.

Wreck it! Down it comes!

Major and Minor

Many songs are composed using pitches from a major or minor scale.

Listen to the major and minor scales that begin on D then sing them with pitch syllables.

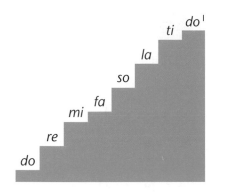

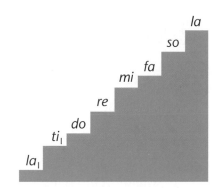

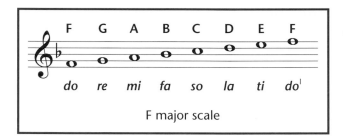

F major scale

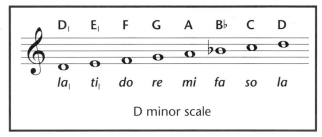

D minor scale

Analyze the pitches of this song to identify the scale.

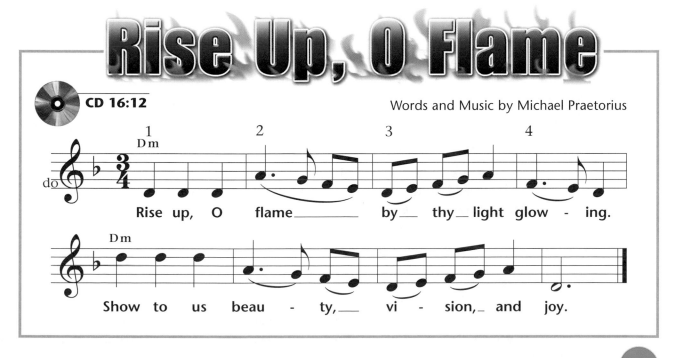

CD 16:12

Words and Music by Michael Praetorius

Rise up, O flame_____ by_ thy_ light glow - ing.

Show to us beau - ty,_ vi - sion,_ and joy.

A Song in Minor

CONCEPT
TONALITY
SKILLS
NAME, SING

Name the minor scale used in this song.

MAP
BRAZIL
PARAGUAY
BOLIVA
CHILE — URUGUAY
ARGENTINA

¿Quién es ese pajarito?

Who Is That Little Bird?

CD 16:18

Argentine Folk Song
English Words by Linda Worsley

Am · F · Em

Spanish: ¿Quién es e - se pa - ja - ri - to que can - ta
Pronunciation: kyen es e se pa xa ɾi to ke kan ta
English: Who is that lit - tle bird sing - ing, Out there in

Em · C · Am

so - bre el li - món? An - da y di - le_____ que no
so βɾel li mon an dai di le ke no
my lem - on tree? Go and tell him_____ stop his

F · Am · E7 · Am

can - te que me ro - ba el co - ra - zón.
kan te ke me ɾo βael ko ɾa son
sing - ing. It_____ takes my heart from me.

Am · F

A - llí_es tá mi_____ nom bre_es - cri - to
a yies ta mi nom bɾes kɾi to
And my name is_____ writ - ten there, oh,

F · Am · E7 · Am

en la ho - ja de_un jaz - mín.
en la o xa ðeun xas min
writ - ten on the jas - mine tree.

Create a Melody in a Minor Key

Read and sing this Russian song in a minor key.

Korobushka

CD 16:21

MAP
KAZAKHSTAN
RUSSIA MONGOLIA
CHINA
INDIA

Russian Folk Song
Russian Words by Nikolay Kekrasov
English Version by MMH

Russian: Ой, пол - на, пол - на ко - ро - буш - ка,
Pronunciation: ɔi pɔl nɑ pɔl nɑ kɔ ɾɔ bush kə
English: "See what I have here in my ko - ro - bush-ka!"

Есть и сит - цы и пар - ча.
yɛst i si tsɪ i pɑɾ cha
We can hear the ped - dler's cry.

По - жа - лей мо - я за - зно - буш - ка
pɔ за lуɛ mɑ yɑ za zno bush kə
"I am on - ly a rag - ged ped - dler, but
Lace and sat - in and col - ored rib - bon, and

Мо - ло - дец - ко го пле - ча.
mɑ lɑ dуɛts kɑ vɔ plуɛ cha
I have trea - sures you can buy:
shin - y beads to catch your eye!"

Create your own minor melody using rhythms from the first two lines of this song.

A Russian Melody in Minor

Read and sing this folk song in E minor.

The Birch Tree

CD 16:25

Russian Folk Song

Russian: Во по-ле бе-рё-за сто-я-ла,
Pronunciation: vo po le be ɣo za sto ya la
English: In the field there stands a leaf-y birch tree.

Во по-ле куд-ря-ва-я сто-я-ла.
vo po le kud ɣya va ya sto ya la
I will make three flutes from its branch-es.

Лю-ли, лю-ли, сто-я-ла!
lyu li lyu li sto ya la
Lyu-li, Lyu-li, I'll make them.

Лю-ли, лю-ли, сто-я-ла!
lyu li lyu li sto ya la
Lyu-li, Lyu-li, from its branch-es.

Piotr Ilyich Tchaikovsky used an arrangement of this folk song in his fourth symphony. Compare Tchaikovsky's version of the melody with the song.

286

Symphony No. 4, Fourth Movement
by Piotr Ilyich Tchaikovsky

This movement starts off in a victorious mood. "The Birch Tree" melody is heard in a variety of ways, sometimes just as a fast fragment. Before the end, the "Fate" theme from the first movement interrupts the victorious mood.

Listen and follow the listening map to hear "The Birch Tree" melody and how it changes.

Listening Map for Symphony No. 4

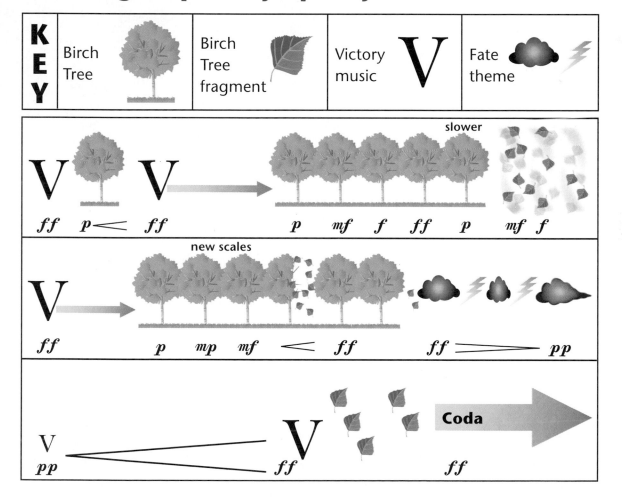

Spotlight on Performance

Spotlight on Performance

Spotlight on Performance

Libretto/Vocal Book (Script)

Scene 1: The New York City Orphanage

NARRATOR 1: The time is 1933.

NARRATOR 2: We're smack dab in the middle of the Great Depression in the city of New York.

NARRATOR 3: It is 4 A.M. at the New York City Orphanage.

(ANNIE has a flashlight and is trying to run away from the orphanage.)

KATE: Annie, what are you doing?

ANNIE: Runnin' away.

JULY: Annie, you're crazy. Miss Hannigan'll catch you.

ANNIE: I don't care. I'm getting outta here.

(MISS HANNIGAN enters and catches her.)

MISS HANNIGAN: Aha! Caught you! Get up and do your chores! Make this dump shine like the top of the Chrysler Building.

IT'S THE HARD-KNOCK LIFE

CD 17:1

Music by Charles Strouse
Words by Martin Charnin

All Orphans

It's the hard-knock life for us!
Got no folks to speak of, so,

It's the hard-knock life for us! 'Stead-a treat-ed,
It's the hard-knock row we hoe! Cot-ton blan-kets

All Orphans *Annie* *All Orphans*

we get tricked! 'Stead-a kiss-es, we get kicked!
'stead-a wool! Emp-ty bel-lies 'stead-a full!

Annie

It's the hard-knock life! Don't it

Kate & Tessie

feel like the wind is al-ways howl-in'? Don't it

Duffy & July

seem like there's nev-er an-y light? Once a

Molly & Pepper

day, don't you wan-na throw the towel in? It's

All Orphans

eas-i-er than put-tin' up a fight. No one's

More

293

there when your dreams at night get creep - y!_____ No one

cares if you grow or if you shrink! No one

dries when your eyes get wet an' weep - y!_____ From the

cry - in', you would think this place-'d sink! Ohhhh!!!!

Emp-ty - bel - ly life! Rot-ten, smel - ly life!

Molly

Full-of-sor-row life! No to-mor-row life! San - ta Claus, we

Pepper

nev - er see. "San - ta Claus," what's that? Who's he?

All Orphans

No one cares for you a smidge when you're in an

or - phan-age! It's the hard - knock life, it's the hard - knock

life, it's the hard - knock life!_____

NARRATOR 1: While everyone at the orphanage was busy cleaning, Annie escaped into the streets of New York.

Scene 2: A Downtrodden Neighborhood Street

DOGCATCHER: You seen any stray dogs around here?

ANNIE: No, sir.

DOGCATCHER: Good. Then they must all be runnin' wild a few streets over.

(The DOGCATCHER EXITS STAGE LEFT; ANNIE notices a DOG OFFSTAGE RIGHT.)

ANNIE: Hey, there's one they didn't get.

(ANNIE gets down on her hands and knees and signals for the DOG to come to her; SANDY, crawling, ENTERS from STAGE RIGHT and CROSSES to ANNIE.)

ANNIE: They're after you, ain't they? Well, they're after me, too. But don't worry, I ain't gonna let them get you or me. Everything's gonna be fine. For the both of us. If not today, well …

Tomorrow

CD 17:2

Music by Charles Strouse
Words by Martin Charnin

Annie

The sun-'ll come out_____ to-mor-row.

Bet your bot-tom dol-lar that to-mor-row,_____ there'll be

sun! Just think-in' a-bout_____ to-mor-row **More**

LIEUTENANT WARD: Hey you! Little girl. Come here.

ANNIE: Yes, Officer?

LIEUTENANT WARD: You're that runaway orphan Miss Hannigan reported. Come with me, I'm taking you back!

(WARD takes ANNIE by the arm and leads her OFFSTAGE. As they EXIT, ANNIE motions for SANDY to follow along.)

NARRATOR 2: Lieutenant Ward took Annie back to the orphanage.

Scene 3: Back at the Orphanage

NARRATOR 3: That afternoon the orphanage received an unusual visitor …

(GRACE FARRELL ENTERS, carrying a briefcase.)

GRACE: Good afternoon. Miss Hannigan?

MISS HANNIGAN: Yes?

GRACE: I'm Grace Farrell, private secretary to Oliver Warbucks.

(GRACE sits in the office chair, STAGE LEFT of the desk.)

MISS HANNIGAN: Oliver Warbucks the millionaire?

GRACE: No, Oliver Warbucks the billionaire. Mr. Warbucks has decided to invite an orphan to spend the Christmas holidays at his home.

MISS HANNIGAN: What sort of orphan did he have in mind?

GRACE: Well, she should be friendly.

(ANNIE waves to GRACE.)

GRACE: And cheerful.

(ANNIE laughs.)

GRACE: And oh, I almost forgot: Mr. Warbucks prefers redheaded children.

MISS HANNIGAN: A cheerful redhead? Sorry, we don't have any orphans like that.

NARRATOR 1: But Grace insisted that Annie be the chosen orphan.

NARRATOR 2: And Annie was off to the Warbucks mansion!

Scene 4: The Warbucks Mansion

NARRATOR 3: Welcome to the Warbucks mansion.

(GRACE and ANNIE ENTER through the door. ANNIE is wearing a new hat and a new coat.)

DRAKE: Good afternoon, Miss Farrell.

GRACE: Good afternoon, Drake. *(To EVERYONE.)* Everyone. This is Annie and her dog, Sandy. *(To ANNIE.)* Annie, this is everyone.

ANNIE: Hi, everyone.

GRACE: Now, what do you want to do first?

ANNIE: The floors. I'll scrub them first; then I'll get to the windows.

DRAKE: Annie, you won't have to do any cleaning. You're our guest.

Annie Junior, Enrico Fermi
Elementary School, Yonkers, NY

GRACE: And, for the next two weeks, you're going to have a swell time. Now …

I Think I'm Gonna Like It Here

CD 17:3

Music by Charles Strouse
Words by Martin Charnin

Grace & Servants
Ce - cille will pick out all your clothes.____ Your bath is drawn by Mis - sus Greer.____ An - nette comes in to make your

Annie
bed.____ I think I'm gon - na like it

Grace & Servants
here! When you wake, ring for Drake. Drake will bring your tray. When you're through, Mis - sus Pugh comes to take it a - way.____

Grace & Half of the Servants
We've nev - er had a lit - tle girl.____

Other Servants
We've nev - er had a lit - tle

More

299

Annie: I'm ver-y glad to vol-un-teer.

girl.

Grace & Servants: We hope you un-der-stand your wish is our com-mand.

We know you're gon-na like it

here. Wel-come!

Scene 4: The Warbucks Mansion (continued)

WARBUCKS: *(From OFFSTAGE RIGHT.)*
Where is everybody?
*(OLIVER WARBUCKS ENTERS with his CHAUFFEUR.
WARBUCKS is carrying a briefcase and
the CHAUFFEUR is carrying two suitcases.)*
Hello, everybody. Drake, dismiss the staff.

DRAKE: Yes, sir.

(The SERVANTS, not including GRACE, EXIT; WARBUCKS turns to speak to GRACE. NOTE: At this point the SERVANTS could change to become an array of New Yorkers.)

WARBUCKS: Well, Annie, I guess we ought to do something special on your first night. *(Has an idea.)* Would you like to go to a movie?

ANNIE: Gosh, Mr. Warbucks, I've never been to one.

WARBUCKS: *(Calls OFFSTAGE LEFT.)* Drake!

DRAKE: *(From OFFSTAGE LEFT.)* Yes, sir?

WARBUCKS: Get our coats. We're going to the movies!

ANNIE: Leapin' lizards!

(DRAKE ENTERS with three coats.)

DRAKE: Which car will you be wanting, sir?

WARBUCKS: This child's been cooped up in an orphanage. We'll walk.

(DRAKE helps WARBUCKS into his coat.)

NARRATOR 2: Oliver Warbucks and Grace showed Annie a part of New York she'd never known before.

N.Y.C.

CD 17:4

Music by Charles Strouse
Words by Martin Charnin

C.   The whole world keeps com - ing,

by   bus,   by train;   you can't   ex - plain

their yen   for   N.   Y.

(ALL FREEZE as one by one, three NARRATORS step forward.)

NARRATOR 1: This was the beginning of many adventures for Little Orphan Annie.

NARRATOR 2: The nation may have been depressed that Christmas of 1933 ...

NARRATOR 3: ... but Annie gave everyone she met, rich or poor, the gift of hope and goodwill.

(EVERYONE unfreezes.)

Annie Junior, Enrico Fermi Elementary School, Yonkers, NY

YOU'RE NEVER FULLY DRESSED WITHOUT A SMILE

CD 17:5

Music by Charles Strouse
Words by Martin Charnin

Hey, ho - bo man,

hey, Dap - per Dan, you've both got your style, but, bro - ther, you're

nev - er ful - ly dressed with - out a smile!

Your clothes may be Beau Brum - mel - ly, they stand out a

mile, but, bro - ther, you're nev - er ful - ly dressed with - out a

smile! Who cares what they're wear - ing on

Main Street or Sa - ville Row? It's what you wear from ear to

ear, and not from head to toe, that mat - ters.

So Sen - a - tor, so jan - i - tor, so long for a

33 while. Re-mem - ber, you're nev - er ful - ly dressed, though

36 you may wear your best. You're nev - er ful - ly

39 dressed with - out a smile!

42 Smile! Smile!! Smile, darn ya, smile!

★ CURTAIN CALL

Meet the Musicians

Annie Junior, Brown University School Adoption Program

Book by:
Thomas Meehan

Thomas Meehan began his career by writing comic stories for magazines such as *The New Yorker*. In addition to *Annie*, Mr. Meehan has written scripts for the musicals *The Producers* and *Hairspray*. He has also written screenplays for movies.

Lyrics by:
Martin Charnin

Martin Charnin started his career with a role in *West Side Story*. Mr. Charnin is also a director, composer, and lyricist. He has worked on more than seventy-five shows.

Music by:
Charles Strouse

Charles Strouse's first Broadway musical was *Bye, Bye Birdie*. His other musicals include *It's a Bird, It's a Plane, It's Superman; Golden Boy;* and *Annie's* sequel, *Annie Warbucks*.

CONCEPT
RHYTHM

SKILLS
SING

If you love to dance, "The Loco-Motion" is the perfect song for you. The song has great dance moves that go with the song. All you need to do is read the words to learn the moves.

SKILL BUILDER: Beat in Your Feet

Speak the syncopated rhythm in the example below. Then tap your feet to the beat.

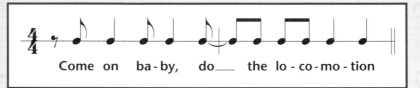

Come on ba - by, do___ the lo - co - mo - tion

The Loco-Motion

CD 17:25

Words and Music by
Gerry Goffin and Carole King

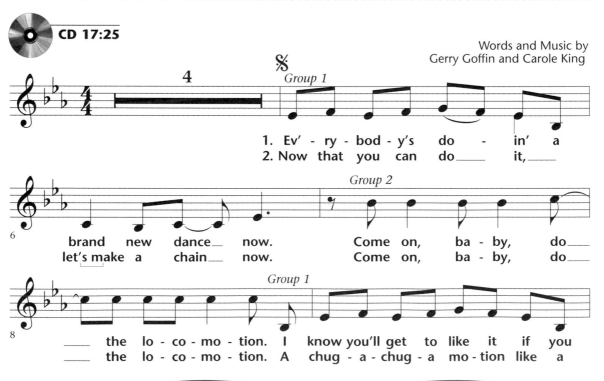

Group 1

1. Ev' - ry - bod - y's do - in' a
2. Now that you can do___ it,___

Group 2

brand new dance___ now. Come on, ba - by, do___
let's make a chain___ now. Come on, ba - by, do___

Group 1

___ the lo - co - mo - tion. I know you'll get to like it if you
___ the lo - co - mo - tion. A chug - a - chug - a mo - tion like a

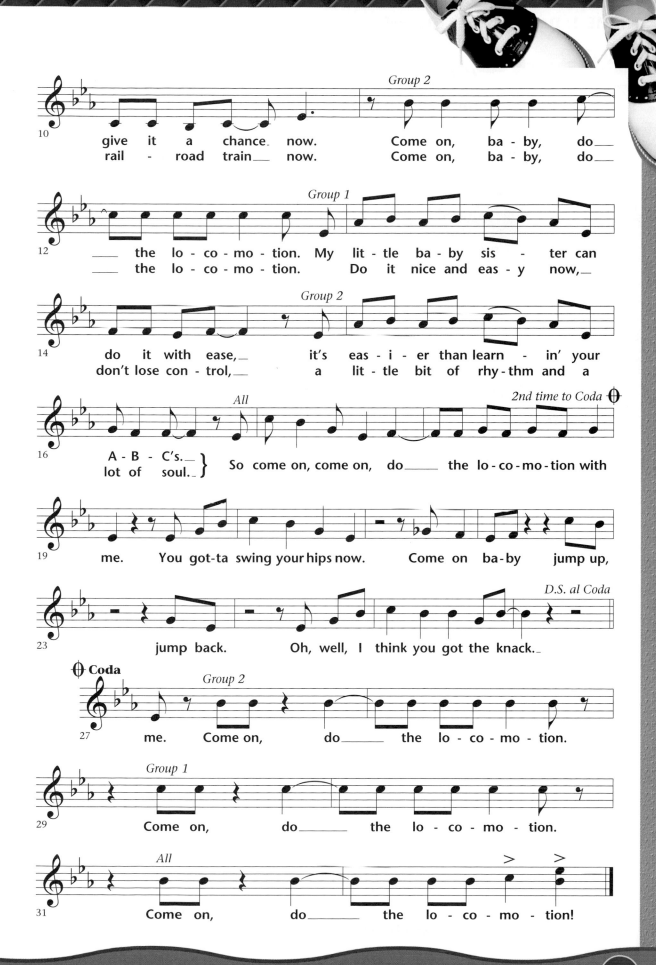

It's a Kid's World

What is it like being a kid? You have times when you need to be serious, like when you do your homework. There are also times when you can relax. Being a kid isn't always easy, but it definitely can be a lot of fun!

Have you ever waited and waited for a special day to come? When that day finally comes, you can't wait to jump out of bed and get the day started. "The New Day" is the perfect song to start one of these great, new days.

"The New Day" is a three-part round. This means there are three groups of singers. When performing a round, each group sings the same melody, but starts at different times.

The New Day

CD 18:4

Anonymous

The new day is dawn-ing, let's greet it with danc-ing. The

hills and_ the_ moun-tains with shep - herd_ tunes_ ring - ing. Hey

tu - li tu - li tu - li tu - la, hey tu - li tu - li tu - li ho!

Have you ever imagined that you could fly? In a book called *The Snowman*, one boy's dream of flying comes true. He builds a snowman who takes him on a flight high over his town. "Walking in the Air" is a song about their magical trip.

VOICE BUILDER: Clear Vocal Tone

How would you feel flying through the air on a cold, winter night? Put this feeling in your voice as you sing the exercise below. Use a light and clear voice. Then **sing** "Walking in the Air" with this same vocal tone.

CD 18:7

Music and Lyrics by Howard Blake
Arranged by Audrey Snyder

peo-ple far be-low are sleep-ing as we fly._____ I'm

hold-ing ver-y tight,_____ I'm rid-ing in the mid-night

I'm hold-ing ver-y tight, I'm rid-ing in the mid-night

blue._____ I'm find-ing I can fly so high a-bove with you.__

On a-cross the world, the vil-lag-es go by like dreams, the
surf-ing in the air, we're swim-ming in the fro-zen sky, we're

riv-ers and the hills, the for-ests and the streams.__
drift-ing o-ver i-cy moun-tains float-ing by.__

Chil-dren gaze o-pen mouthed, tak-en by sur-prise.

Chil-dren gaze, ah_____

 **LISTENING** CD 18:10

Walking in the Air by Howard Blake

The King's Singers are a group of six men from England who sing classical and popular songs.

Listen to their performance of "Walking in the Air." How is their version similar to the one you sing?

CONCEPT
MELODY
SKILLS
SING

The words to "The Swing" are from a book of poems written by Robert Louis Stevenson called *A Child's Garden of Verses*. These poems are about things children liked to do in the 1800s. More than 100 years later, you probably enjoy doing some of the same things.

VOICE BUILDER: High to Low

When you play on a swing you go up and down. Your voice does the same thing when you sing.

Practice the melody in the exercise. What direction does it move?

Ah ____
Up   in   the   air   so   blue ____
Up   in   the   air   and   down ____

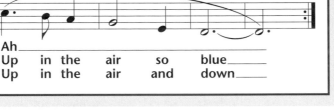

The Swing

CD 18:11

Music by John Chorbajian
Words by Robert Louis Stevenson
from *A Child's Garden of Verses*

Moderately, with motion

How   do   you   like   to   go   up   in   a   swing,

up   in   the   air   so   blue? ____   Oh,   I   do

think   it   the   pleas - ant - est   thing   ev - er   a   child   can

Our Musical Lives

The sounds of music fill our lives. Music from a clock radio might wake you up in the morning. You might put headphones on to listen to music on the way to school. You probably listen to or play music at parties with your friends and family. If you watch television, you hear music in nearly every program. When it's time for bed, music might even help you fall to sleep. We really do have musical lives!

VOICE BUILDER: Project Your Voice

Have you ever called to a friend across a playground or field? You may notice your voice carries farther when you project your voice at a high pitch.

Sing this melody and project your voice as if you were calling someone far away. Repeat it at higher and lower pitch levels.

Hey you! Hey you! Hey you!
Wake up! Wake up! Wake up!

Wake Up Canon

CD 18:18

American Folk Song

Now all the woods are wak - ing, the sun is ris - ing high. Wake up now, get up now, be - fore the dew is dry.

CONCEPT
EXPRESSION
SKILLS
SING

"Ogguere" is a beautiful lullaby from Cuba that celebrates the birth of a prince named Ogguere. He lived in the country of Nigeria in West Africa, a place where the ancestors of many Cubans came from. The words are in an Afro-Cuban dialect of Spanish. They describe Ogguere's mother telling him to go to sleep because she has many things to do.

VOICE BUILDER: Expression

In a lullaby, the singer gradually sings softer as the baby is going to sleep. Singing softly is a type of **expression**. Expression is the way a musician puts feeling into a song.

Sing this exercise three times. Sing more softly each time through. Hum the tune on the last time.

Repeat 3 times

mp - p 1.-2. O - ggue - re, o - ggue - re, o - ggue - re.
pp   3. hmm

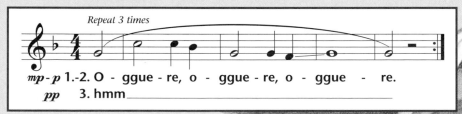

MAP
FLORIDA
CUBA
HAITI
DOMINICAN
REPUBLIC

Ogguere

CD 18:21

An Afro-Cuban Cradle Song
by Gilberto Valdés
Arranged by Carlos R. Abril

Afro-Cuban Spanish: **O - ggue - re,   o - ggue - re,   o - ggue -**
(Dialect)
Pronunciation: o   ge   ɾe   o   ge   ɾe   o   ge

12   re   o - ggue - re,   o - ggue - re,   o - ggue -
      ɾe   o   ge   ɾe   o   ge   ɾe   o   ge

More

Choral Songs to Perform   327

16 re La cam - pa - na la sei_____ ta re - so - na ba -
    ɾe la kam pa na la sei ta ɾe so na βa

19 tey_____ y la gen - te do - ta - sion Va re -
    tei i lo xen te ðo ta syon ba ɾe

24 sá la o - ra - sion_____ O -
    sa lo ɾa syon o

30 ggue - re, o - ggue - re, o - ggue - re o - ggue - re, o -
    ge ɾe o ge ɾe o ge ɾe o ge ɾe o

35 ggue - re, o - ggue - re O - ggue - re dru - me -
    ge ɾe o ge ɾe o ge ɾe ðɾu me

38 ri_____ que yo tien que su - sí_____
    ɾi ke yo tyen ke su si

The waterfront in
Havana, Cuba

(328)

41   Y di - pué___ ja - sé e - co pa com - prá ba - rra -
   i ði pwe   ya se e ko pa kom pra βa ɾa

46   cón   O -
  kon   o

61   ggue - re, o - ggue - re, o - ggue - re O-ggue-re dru - me -
  ge - ɾe o ge ɾe o ge ɾe o ge ɾe ðɾu me

65   ri___   Que yo tien que su - sí
  ɾi   ke yo tyen ke su si

68   O - ggue - re, o - ggue - re, o - ggue - o-
  o - ge ɾe o ge ɾe o ge o

gradual rit.

73   hmm___   hmm___

 **LISTENING**   CD 18:25

Ogguere An Afro-Cuban Lullaby

Listen to the Bebo Valdés Trio perform "Ogguere."
In their version of the song, they do not sing the words.
What instrument do you hear playing the melody?

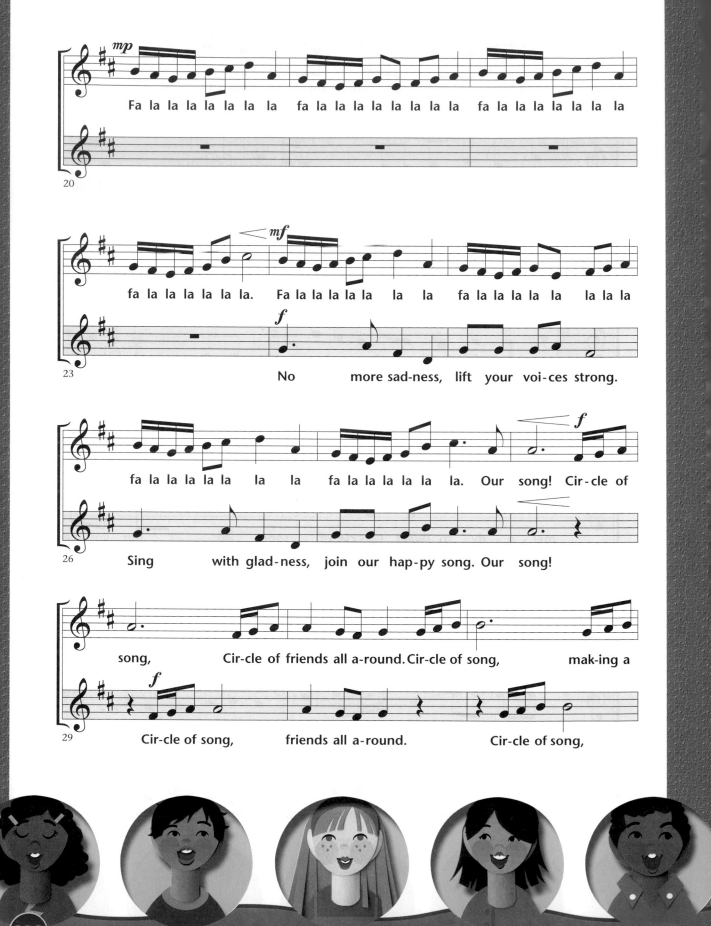

clear and joy - ful sound. Cir - cle of song,_____ we lift our

clear and joy - ful sound. Cir - cle of song, we lift our

voi - ces now to say, Cir - cle of song will bright - en ev - 'ry

voi - ces now to say, Cir - cle of song will bright - en ev - 'ry

(All) **_mf_**

day. Our song will bright - en ev - 'ry day.

CONCEPT
MELODY

SKILLS
SING

"**D**on't Let the Music Stop" gives your choir the chance to sing in two parts. You will learn to sing each part separately. When you hear them sung together, you won't want the music to stop!

VOICE BUILDER: High and Low

Sing both high and low pitches in this exercise that comes from "Don't Let the Music Stop."

Repeat at higher pitches

Ah_____   Oh_____
I   hear   sing - ing.

CD 19:1

Words and Music by
Eugene Butler

1st and 3rd times

Don't let   the mu - sic   stop,—   let's

2nd and 3rd times

I   hear_____   A - mer - i - ca

keep   it   firm and   strong;   Don't   let   the

sing - ing,   I   hear   her   sing - ing,   Var - ied

Nature's Songs

If you take a walk through the woods, the music of the natural world fills your ears. You might hear a gurgling stream, the cry of an eagle in the sky, or the whoosh of the wind through the trees. In this theme, you will sing songs that all express the beauty of the natural world.

VOICE BUILDER: Singing Long Phrases

Practice this breathing exercise to expand your breathing capacity. This will improve your ability to sing longer phrases.

- Imagine you have a milkshake as large as the room. "Drink" the air through a giant straw.
- Imagine there is an elevator at the bottom of your lungs. Take the elevator from the basement to the first floor over 4 counts.

Now can you sing this full musical phrase in one breath?

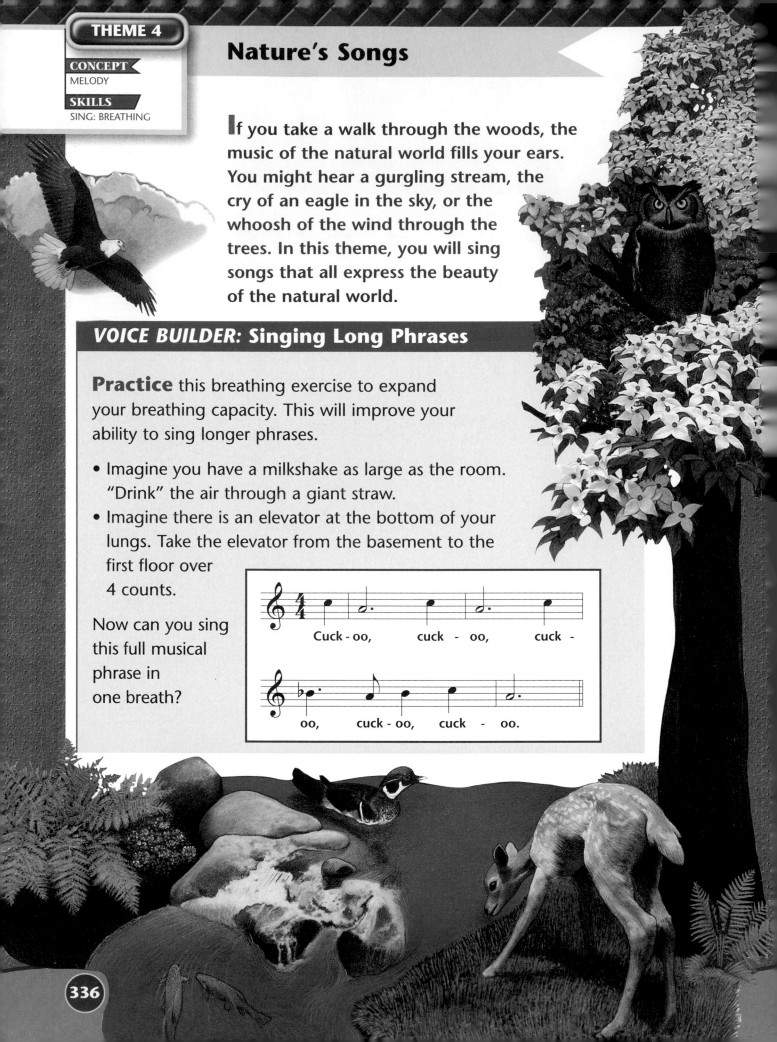

Cuck - oo,   cuck - oo,   cuck -

oo,   cuck - oo,   cuck - oo.

The flight of a bird moves up and down like the melody of a song. As you sing the two rounds below, imagine your voice is a bird flying through the air. When the melody goes up, your voice soars toward the clouds. When the melody goes down, your voice floats to the ground.

E A G L E

CD 19:5

Music by Moritz Hauptmann (adapted)
Words by MMH

Andantino, legato

Wheel - ing and turn - ing, an ea - gle in flight Will

fly a - way, will fly a - way, will soar out of sight.

The Owl and the Cuckoo

CD 19:8

Anonymous

We hear the night owl call - ing from for - est still and

dark, While from the tall - est oak tree the cuck - oo an - swers

back: Cuck - oo, cuck - oo, cuck - oo, cuck-oo, cuck -

oo. Cuck - oo, cuck - oo, cuck - oo, cuck-oo, cuck - oo.

CONCEPT
MELODY

SKILLS
SING: CHORAL BLEND

After a visit to the mountains of the Hawaiian island of Moloka'i, Herb Mahelona wrote a song to ask people to help take special care of nature.

VOICE BUILDER: Blend Your Voice

Blend your voice with others by matching your vowel sounds. The five basic vowels are *ee, eh, ah, oh, oo.* **Sing** vowels with a relaxed jaw, vertical mouth shape, and space inside the mouth.

loo loo loo loo loo	loo,	loo loo loo loo loo_____	loo
la la la la la	la,	la la la la la_____	la
le - le wa - le la - kou,		le - le wa - le la -	kou

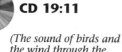

E nānā kākou i nā manu

Look at the Birds in the Sky

CD 19:11

(The sound of birds and the wind through the ironwood trees.)

Words and Music by Herb Mahelona

Hawaiian: 1. E nā - nā kā - kou i nā___ ma - nu i nā___ ma - nu
Pronunciation: ε na na ka kou i na mʌ nu i na mʌ nu

2. E nā - nā kā - kou i kō___ lā - kou, i kō___ lā - kou
   ε na na ka kou i ko la kou i ko la kou

ma ka___ la - ni.   }   Ma - lu - na lo - a   o ka ho - nu - a,
mʌ kʌ lʌ ni   mʌ lu nʌ lo ʌ   o kʌ ho nu ʌ

kī - ka - ha 'a - na. }
ki kʌ hʌ 'ʌ nʌ

1.   2.

le - le wa - le lā - kou, le - le wa - le lā - kou.   le - le wa - le lā -
lε lε vʌ lε la kou   lε lε vʌ lε la kou   lε lε vʌ lε lʌ

CONCEPT
RHYTHM
SKILLS
SING

The Spanish words to the song "Arroyito serrano" describe a little mountain stream. The stream's beautiful song calls a person to come and hear its sweet music.

Arroyito serrano

CD 19:15

Mountain Stream

Words and Music by
Carlos Guastavino

Allegretto

Spanish: **A** - rro - yi - to   se - rra - no___   **Que**
Pronunciation: a   ɾo   yi   to   se   ɾa   no   ke

Spanish: **To** - das las   ma - ña - ni - tas___   **Me**
Pronunciation: to   ðas las   ma   nya   ni   tas   me

vie - nes ba - jan - do͜ha - cia͜el   lla - no,___   A - gua cla - ri - ta
βye   nes   βa   xan   doa   syel   ʒa   no   a   gwa klɑ   ɾi   ta

lla - ma   tu   can - to   le - ja - no,___   Ven - go   co - rrien - do͜a
ya   ma   tu   kan   to   le   xa   no   beng   go   ko   ɾyen   ðoa

tra - es.___   Per - fu - me   de   miel   y   de͜a - zaha - res.___
tɾa   es   peɾ   fu   me   ðe   myel   i   ðea   sa   ɾes

ver - te___   Que - ri - do͜a - rro - yi - to   se - rra - no.___
βeɾ   te   ke   ɾi   ðoa   ɾo   yi   to   se   ɾa   no

Arroyito serrano by Carlos Guastavino

Listen to "Arroyito serrano" performed by the Indiana University Children's Choir. Performing in a children's choir requires dedication and a commitment to practice. The excitement of singing and performing makes the hard work worth it.

CONCEPT
MELODY

SKILLS
SING

"**O**ver the Sea to Skye" describes a narrow escape to sea after a battle on land. Though the waves are rough, the sea is a safe place for the people in the song.

Over the Sea to Skye

CD 19:24

Music by Annie MacLeod
Words by Sir Harold Boulton

Refrain

"Speed, bon-nie boat, like a bird on the wing:
"Car - ry the lad that's born to be king

On - ward! the sail - ors cry!_____
O - ver the sea to Skye!"

Verse

1. Loud the winds howl, loud the waves roar,
2. Tho the waves leap, soft shall ye sleep,
3. Man - y's the lad fought on that day,
4. Burned are our homes, ex - ile and death

Thun - der clouds rend the air;_____ Baf - fled our foes,
O - cean's a roy - al bed;_____ Rocked in the deep,
Well the clay more could wield,_____ When the night came,
Scat - ter the loy - al men;_____ Yet ere the sword

Last time to Refrain and end at Fine

stand on the shore, Fol - low they will not dare._____
flo - ra will keep Watch by your wea - ry head._____
si - lent - ly lay Dead on Cul - lo - den's field._____
cool in the sheath, Char - lie will come a - gain._____

CONCEPT
MELODY
SKILLS
SING, READ

Trips are often filled with exciting experiences. However, they can make you feel homesick, too. In the Japanese words to "Hitori," a young girl sadly sings as she thinks about the beautiful cherry trees at her home in Japan.

VOICE BUILDER: Legato

Sing the exercise below in a smooth, **legato** style. Legato is marked in music notation with a long, curving arc. Look for legato marks in "Hitori," and then sing the song using legato style.

do re mi so la do¹ la so mi re do

Hitori

Japanese Folk Song
Additional Lyrics and Arrangement by
Mary Donnelly and George L.O. Strid

CD 19:27

Gentle rocking
10
All - Unison
_mp_

Japanese:	ひ と___ り で せ び しぃ	ふ た り で
Pronunciation:	hI to ɾi dɑ sɑ bi shi	fu tɑ ɾi de
English: (optional)	**Here am__ I,** so all a-lone	dream-ing of the

14

ま い り ま しょ	ひ と 、 り で せ び しぃ
mɑ i ɾi mɑ sho	hi to ɾi de sɑ bi shi
cher-ry trees of home.	Here am__ I, so all a-lone

More

ふ た り で ま い り ま しょ

fu ta ri de ma i ri ma sho

dream-ing of the cher-ry trees of home.

Part I

1. There by the riv-er sits a pret-ty maid-en watch-ing the wa-ter
2. Now, as the moon-light dan-ces on the riv - er, sad-ly the maid-en

Part II (1st time only)

Slow - ly mov - ing. Mov - ing

move a-long. She sees a love-ly blos-som-ing cher-ry tree
must de-part. Each gen-tle breeze that sighs_ through the cher-ry tree

slow. Slow - ly mov - ing.

and her_ heart is filled with song. "Some day I will_ go
ech-oes the song that fills her heart.

Mov - ing slow. "Some day I will go

to my home that I love_ so. Once more I will_ be

to my home that I love so. Once more I will be

'neath the love-ly cher - ry tree."

'neath the love-ly cher - ry tree."

2.

"Some day I will__ go to my home that

"Some day I will__ go

I love__ so. Once more I will__ be

to my home that I love__ so. Once more

D.S. al Fine

'neath the love-ly cher - ry tree." __

I will__ be 'neath the love-ly cher - ry tree."

CONCEPT
EXPRESSION

SKILLS
SING

In certain parts of the mountains of Peru, people celebrate the Yunza Festival, or Festival of Joy, in February or March. At this festival, people fill a hollow tree trunk with gifts. People take turns chopping the trunk until it falls and the gifts spill out onto the ground. "La Yunsita" is a song people sing at the festival.

VOICE BUILDER: Expressive Singing

Expressive singing can make your performance more beautiful.

Sing this vocal exercise, which is based on the refrain of "La Yunsita." Then use your voice in a light and dance-like way to sing the song.

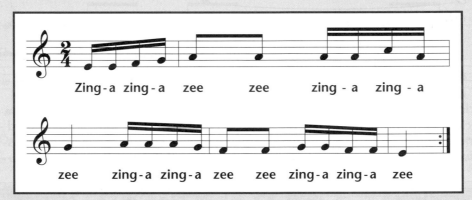

Zing-a zing-a zee   zee   zing-a zing-a
zee   zing-a zing-a zee   zee zing-a zing-a zee

La Yunsita

MAP

PERU   BRAZIL
BOLIVA
CHILE
ARGENTINA

CD 20:5

Arranged by
Rosa Mercedes Ayarza de Morales

Allegro   8   Verse

Spanish: 1. Yun - si - ta, yun - si - ta,   yun - si - ta, yun - si - ta,
Pronunciation: yun   si   ta yun si   ta   yun   si   ta yun si   ta
Spanish: 2. Sau - ce - si - to ver - de,   sau - ce - si - to ver - de,
Pronunciation: sau se   si to βer ðe   sau se   si to βer ðe

13 ¿Quién te tum - ba - rá? ¡Ja jay! ¿Quién te tum - ba - rá? ¡Ja jay!
kyen te tum ba ɾa xa xai kyen te tum ba ɾa xa xai

¿Qué ha-ces en la playa? ¡Ja jay! ¿Qué ha-ces en la playa? ¡Ja jay!
kea ses en la playa xa xai kea ses en la playa xa xai

17 Y el que te tum - ba - re, y el que te tum - ba - re,
yel ke te tum ba ɾe yel ke te tum ba ɾe

Prés - ta - me tu som - bra, prés - ta - me tu som - bra,
pɾes ta me tu som bɾa pɾes ta me tu som bɾa

Refrain

21 Te re - no - va - rá, ¡Ja jay! Te re - no - va - rá.
te ɾe no βa ɾa xa xai te ɾe no βa ɾa

Has - ta que me vaya ¡Ja jay! Has - ta que me vaya.
as ta ke me βaya xa xai as ta ke me βaya

} Hua - chi - gua-
wa chi gwa

25 li - to, hua - chi - gua - ló, pa - ra a - mar - te ¡Só - lo yo! Hua - chi - gua-
li to wa chi gwa lo pa ɾa mar te so lo yo wa chi gwa

4

29 li - to, hua - chi - gua - ló, pa - ra a - mar - te ¡Só - lo yo!
li to wa chi gwa lo pa ɾa mar te so lo yo

The ruins of Machu Picchu at sunset, ca. 1995 Peru.

Spotlight on Celebrations

Spotlight on Celebrations

Spotlight on Celebrations

Songs of Our Country

The Reverend Samuel Smith wrote the words to "America" in 1831. Later he chose music from a collection of German melodies and set the words to music. The music comes from "God Save the Queen," the British national anthem.

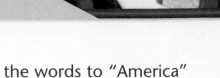

CD 20:10

Music by Henry Carey
Words by Samuel F. Smith

1. My coun - try, 'tis of thee, Sweet land of
2. My na - tive coun - try thee, Land of the
3. Let mu - sic swell the breeze, And ring from
4. Our fa - thers' God, to Thee, Au - thor of

lib - er - ty, Of thee I sing.
no - ble free, Thy name I love.
all the trees Sweet Free - dom's song;
lib - er - ty, To Thee we sing.

Land where my fa - thers died, Land of the Pil - grim's pride,
I love thy rocks and rills, Thy woods and tem - pled hills;
Let mor - tal tongues a - wake, Let all that breathe par - take,
Long may our land be bright With Free-dom's ho - ly light;

From ev - 'ry___ moun - tain - side Let___ free - dom ring.
My heart_ with_ rap - ture thrills Like_ that a - bove.
Let rocks_ their_ si - lence break, The___ sound pro - long.
Pro - tect___ us___ by Thy might, Great_ God, our King!

LISTENING / **CD 20:13**

The Stars and Stripes Forever by John Philip Sousa

"The Stars and Stripes Forever" is a piece written for band. John Philip Sousa composed this piece on Christmas in 1896. It is the official march of the United States of America.

Listen to the different instruments playing in this band.

Listening Map for
The Stars and Stripes Forever

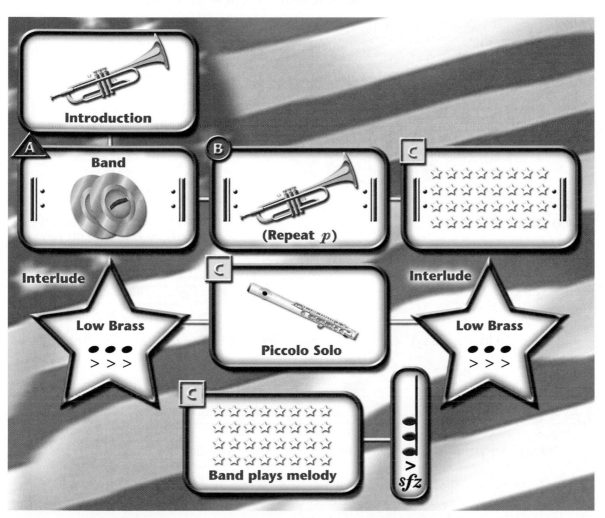

CONCEPT
BEAT/METER

SKILLS
LISTEN, PLAY

During the War of 1812, Francis Scott Key watched as the British attacked Fort McHenry in Baltimore. After the smoke had cleared, he saw the flag still waving in the breeze. He was inspired to write the words to "The Star-Spangled Banner." The words were later set to music and "The Star-Spangled Banner" was declared the national anthem of the United States.

As you listen to "The Star-Spangled Banner" tap your foot on the first beat of each measure and clap on beats two and three.

The Star-Spangled Banner

CD 20:14

Music Attributed to J.S. Smith
Words by Francis Scott Key

Oh, ___ say! can you see, by the dawn's ear - ly light,

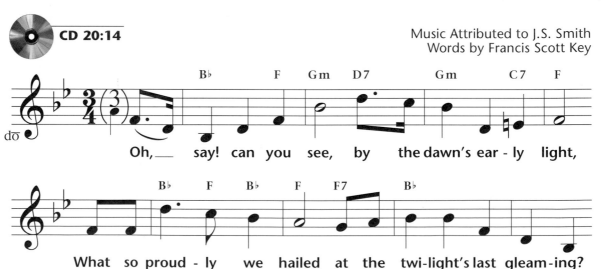

What so proud - ly we hailed at the twi-light's last gleam-ing?

Whose broad stripes and bright stars, through the per-il-ous fight,

O'er the ram-parts we watched were so gal-lant-ly stream-ing?

And the rock-ets' red glare, the bombs burst-ing in air,

Gave proof through the night that our flag was still there.

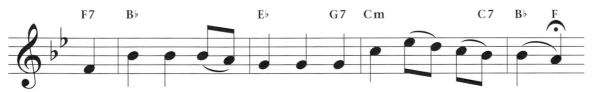

Oh, say, does that_ Star-Span-gled Ban-ner_ yet_ wave_

O'er the land___ of the free and the home of the brave?

People express love for their country by singing songs. Songs bring people together and help them express pride for the country in which they live. "America, My Homeland" describes the beauty of the United States.

America, My Homeland

CD 20:17

Music by Robert de Frece
Words by Robert de Frece and Shirley Funk

A - mer - i - ca, my home - land, _ great land of lib - er - ty,

Where peo - ple live in free - dom _ from sea to shin - ing sea.

Where wav - ing wheat fields grow and gen - tle bree - zes blow,

Where for - ests tall reach up - ward_ to moun - tains capped with snow.

A - mer - i - ca, A - mer - i - ca, we sing our praise to thee,

And proud - ly we sa - lute the flag that flies for you and me!

Sing of America

Words by H. Wilburr

Sing A - mer - i - cans, glad - ly sing

While the bells of free - dom ring!

Hail our flag on land and sea.

Sing that here we all are free!

CONCEPT
DYNAMICS
SKILLS
SING, DESCRIBE

People and events can be honored and remembered in many ways. "We Remember" honors our fallen heroes and reminds us of how we felt as a nation after September 11, 2001.

CD 20:20

Words and Music by
John Jacobson and Mac Huff
Arranged by Mac Huff

There was a day when free-dom's light seemed
day when A-mer-i-cans

ve-ry far a-way.___ There was a day that looked like
chose to take a stand._ There was a day when the best of

night; we dreamed of yes-ter-day.___ But
friends of-fered us their hand.__ The

e-ven when the day is dark_ and rain-bows hard to see,___
world can still be beau-ti-ful___ but e-ven when it's gray,_

her-oes walk a-mong_ us and
the sun will shine up-on___ us and

Identify the dynamic markings in "We Remember."
Perform the song, emphasizing the dynamics.

Hispanic Heritage Month

September 15 to October 15 is National Hispanic Heritage Month. Hispanic Americans celebrate their history and culture with food, dance, and songs of their homeland. Sing this Mexican folk song about love of homeland.

The Village

MAP
UNITED STATES
MEXICO
BELIZE
GUATEMALA

 **CD 20:23**

Mexican Folk Song
English Words by MMH

Spanish: Al pie de un ver-de que-li-te me dio sue-ño y me dor-
Pronunciation: al pye ðe un βeɾ de ke li te me ðyo swe nyoi me ðoɾ
English: **At the edge of a green _ *que - li - te,* I stopped a-while there to**

mí, y me des-per-tó un ga-lli-to can-tan-do "qui qui ri
mi i me ðes peɾ toun ga yi to kan tan do ki ki ɾi
sleep. A roos-ter cried out and woke me. He sang a "qui qui ri

quí." No can-to por-que si pue-da, ni por-que mi voz sea
ki no kan to poɾ ke si pwe ða ni poɾ ke mi βos sea
qui." I don't sing be-cause I'm a-ble, nor be-cause _ my voice is

buena,   can-to por-que ten-go gus-to   en mi tie-rra y en la a-
βwena   kan to por ke teng go gus to   en mi tye ɾa ien la
good._   I sing be-cause_ I feel joy_   in my land_ and for-eign

je - na. Ma - ña - na, me voy ma - ña - na,   ma - ña - na me voy de a-
xe na ma nya na me βoi ma nya na   ma nya na me βoi ðea
lands._ To-mor-row I will be leav-ing, and who can tell where I'll

quí, y el con-sue-lo que me que-da   que se han de a-cor-dar de mí.
ki iel kon swe lo ke me ke ða   ke sean dea koɾ ðaɾ ðe mi
be? But here is my con-so - la-tion: that some - one re-mem-bers me.

Clap the rhythm of the Spanish verse of "El quelite" along
with the recording.

 LISTENING CD 20:27

El tecolote (excerpt) Mexican Folk Song

"El tecolote" ("The Owlet") is a song from the southwest of
Mexico. The song style is called *gusto*.

Identify the group of instruments playing "El tecolote."

 See **music.mmhschool.com** to
research Mexican music.

This Danish harvest song tells about the importance of the harvest time for the farmers. The harvest helps them remember the past as well as celebrate the future.

Use hand signs to identify *high do* and *low do* in this song about harvest time in Denmark.

high do   low do

MAP
NORWAY
FINLAND
SWEDEN
DENMARK
RUSSIA

Marken er mejet

Out in the Meadow

CD 20:28

Danish Folk Song
English Version by MMH

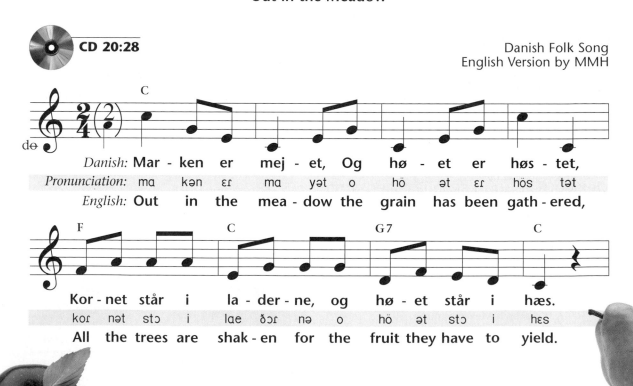

Danish: Mar - ken er mej - et, Og hø - et er høs - tet,
Pronunciation: mɑ kən ɛɹ mɑ yət o hö ət ɛɹ hös tət
English: **Out in the mea - dow the grain has been gath - ered,**

Kor - net står i la - der - ne, og hø - et står i hæs.
koɹ nət stɔ i lɑɛ ðɔɹ nə o hö ət stɔ i hɛs
All the trees are shak - en for the fruit they have to yield.

Rev vi mark - en let, det er gam - mel ret,
ɹeu vi mɑ kən lət de ɛɹ gɑm mel ɹɛt
Now we're on our way, Home - ward bound to stay,

fug - len og den fat - ti - ge skal og - så væ - re maet.
fu lən o dɛn fɑe ti yə ʒkəl ɔs sə ve ɹɑ mɛt
Home to share our boun - ty with the glean-ers of the field.

Art Gallery

The Harvesters

This painting was created by Pieter Brueghel (1525-1569). It shows people in Northern Europe during wheat harvesting time.

CONCEPT
TONALITY

SKILLS
SING, LISTEN

Tết *Trung Thu,* or Mid-Autumn Moon Festival, is one of the most popular festivals in Vietnam. Tết Trung Thu means "Children's Festival." Vietnamese families celebrate their children with many different activities. Children march in parades while singing and carrying colorful handmade lanterns. Vietnamese parents tell their children stories and serve them special treats such as *mooncakes,* which are little cakes with bright yellow centers.

Tết Trung

Children's Festival

MAP

MYANMAR
LAOS
THAILAND
KAMPUCHEA   VIETNAM

CD 21:1

Vietnamese Song
Collected and Transcribed by Kathy B. Sorensen
English Words by MMH

Vietnamese: Tt trung thu rc   dn   di   chi.   Em rc   dn   di   khp phõphng.
Pronunciation: tɛt tɾuŋ tu ɾʊk dɛn di choi   ɛm ɾuk dɛn di kap fo fuŋ
English: 1. At Mid-Au-tumn Fes-ti - val,   walk a - round with lan-terns   lit.
2. Beau-ti - ful and full the moon,   at Mid - Au - tumn Fes - ti - val.

Long   vui sng   vi — dn trong tay   Em múa_ ca trong nh trng   rỜm.
lʌŋ   vuɪ suŋ voɪ   dɛn tɾaŋ taɪ   ɛm muə   ka tɾaŋ ʌn tɾaŋ ɾam
Take them all   a - cross the town,   Sing-ing_ to the   au-tumn moon.
Wait - ing for   the_ moon to rise,   I can_hear the sound of drums,

Dn   ng sao vi   dn   cá chm.   Dn thin nga vi   den bm bm.
dɛn ʌŋ saʊ voɪ   dɛn ka cham   dɛn tiɛn nga voɪ dɛn bʊm bʊm
Lan-terns all   in   dif-f'rent shapes,   Lan-tern an - gel, lan-tern dream,
Tung yin yin kak tung yin   yin,   Tung yin yin kak tung yin yin.

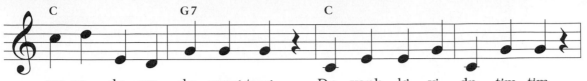

em rɔc dn ny dn cung trng.
ɛm ɾuk dɛn naɪ nɛn kung tɾang
Lan-tern fish, or lan-tern star,
I can hear the sound of drums,

Dn xanh lơ vi dn tim tim.
dɛn sʌn lə voɪ dɛn tim tim
Lan-tern swan or but-ter-fly.
Tung yin yin kak tung yin yin,

Dn xanh lam vi dn trậng trậng,
dɛn sʌn lam voɪ dɛn tɾang tɾang
Take my lan-tern to the sky;
Tung yin yin kak tung yin yin.

trong nh dn rc rở mun mu.
tɾang ʌn dɛn ɾuk ɾʊ mun mau
Take my lan-tern to the moon.
Wel-come, la-dy in the moon!

LISTENING CD 21:5

Qua Cầ Gió Bay Vietnamese Folk Song

The title of this song means "Wind on the Bridge." It is traditionally sung during autumn and spring festivals in Vietnam. Children in Vietnam enjoy listening to and singing this song.

CD-ROM

Use *World Instruments* **CD-ROM** to learn more about Southeast Asian instruments.

CONCEPT
RHYTHM
SKILLS
SING

Ghosts, goblins, and things that go bump in the night bring thrills and chills to Halloween night. Sing this song about a playful ghost.

The Boogie-Woogie Ghost

CD 21:6

Words and Music Nadine M. Peglar

Verse

1. There was a ghost on Hal-low-een, He real-ly made the ghost-ie scene,
2. He'd go out spook-ing late at night, And giv-ing ev-'ry-one a fright,

He was the Boo-gie-Woo-gie Ghost, He was the ghost-ie with the most,
He knew some wit-ches, two or three, And they would all go on a spree,

And when the kid-dies came a-round, He'd give out with a ghost-ly sound,
And when the morn-ing came a-round, He'd give one last mys-te-ri-ous sound,

He'd go,_____ "Boo-oo-oo-oo-ooo."   ooo."

Refrain

Though he real-ly was-n't ver-y spook-y,

Kids all thought that he was rath-er cool.

E-ven though he was a lit-tle kook-y,

He was just a spe-cial ghoul. When you're

out on Hal-low-een And he ap-pears up-on the scene,

Don't give a scream and run a-way, Just ask him if he'll stay and play.

You'll like the Boo-gie-Woo-gie Ghost, He'll be the one you dig the most,

You'll love his Boo - oo - oo - oo - ooo.

CONCEPT
RHYTHM
SKILLS
SING, READ

Thanksgiving is a time of family gatherings. Family members travel long distances to be with relatives for the holidays.

Sing this traditional Thanksgiving song about being together on Thanksgiving Day.

Use body percussion to accompany this song. Tap your left hand on the desk, then your right hand, then clap your hands together.

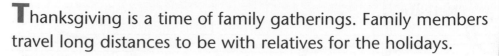

CD 21:9

American Folk Melody
Words by Lydia Maria Childs

1. O - ver the riv - er and through the wood,
2. O - ver the riv - er and through the wood,

To Grand-moth - er's house we go;
Trot fast, my dap - ple gray!

The horse knows the way to car - ry the sleigh
Spring o - ver the ground like a hunt - ing hound,

Through the white and drift - ed snow.
For this is Thanks - giv - ing day!

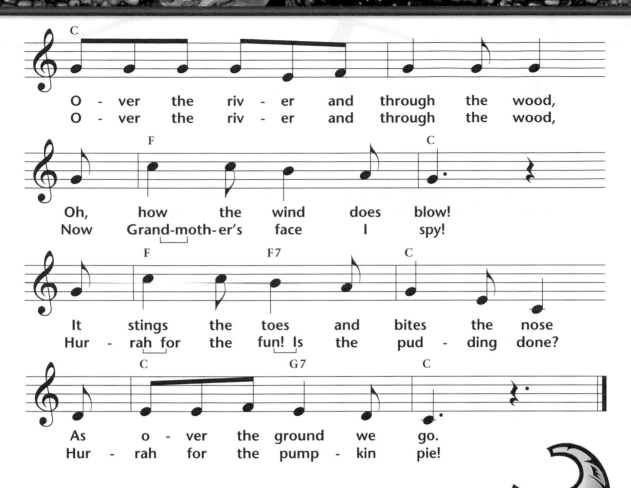

O - ver the riv - er and through the wood,
O - ver the riv - er and through the wood,

Oh, how the wind does blow!
Now Grand-moth-er's face I spy!

It stings the toes and bites the nose
Hur - rah for the fun! Is the pud - ding done?

As o - ver the ground we go.
Hur - rah for the pump - kin pie!

Sing this round about the spirit of Thanksgiving Day, standing up each time you sing the word "Thank," and sitting down on the word "Food."

Song of Thanksgiving

CD 21:12

Words and Music by Robert de Frece

Thank you for our man - y bless - ings,

Food and fam - 'ly, friend - ship true.

CONCEPT
FORM/STRUCTURE
SKILLS
SING, PLAY

During the eight days of Hanukkah, Jewish people around the world celebrate the victory of a small group of people over a great army. Each night, children eagerly help light the candles of the menorah. Families and friends exchange small gifts, eat special foods, and sing songs that tell the Hanukkah story. Children have fun playing with a spinning top called a *dreidel*.

S'vivon Sov
Dreidel Spin

CD 21:18

Hebrew Folk Song
English Words by Linda Worsley

Hebrew: ס - בִּי - בוֹן סוֹב סוֹב סוֹב חַ - נוּ - כָּה טוֹב חַג-הוּא
Pronunciation: sɛ vi von sov sov sov xa nu ka hu xag tov
English: Drei-del spin, drei-del spin, Ha-nuk-kah____ Ha-nuk-kah.

חַ - נוּ - כָּה הוּא חַג טוֹב ס - בִּי - בוֹן סוֹב סוֹב סוֹב
xa nu ka hu xag tov sɛ vi von sov sov sov
Hol - i - day, come and play, drei-del spin,__ spin, spin, spin.

חַג שְׁמֵ-חַה הוּא לָ-עַם נֵס גָ-דוֹל הָ - יָה שָׁם
xag sim xa hu la am nes ga dol ha ya sham
It's a day for all our peo - ple. It's a day when we re-mem-ber

נֵס גָ - דוֹל הָ - יָה שָׁם חַג שִׁמְ-חַה הוּא לָ-עַם
nes ga dol ha ya sham xag sim xa hu la am
when there was a great mir-a-cle. Cel - e-brate this hap-py day!

Play the rhythm patterns to accompany "S'vivon Sov."

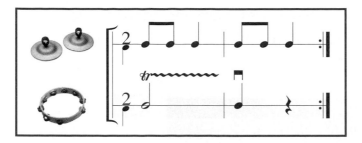

 Art Gallery

La Vie

La Vie was created by Marc Chagall (1887-1985). This part of the painting shows musicians and performers in a scene that could be from the circus. *La vie* means "life" in French. Why do you think he gave the painting this title?

Las posadas is a Christmas celebration in Mexico and in parts of the southern United States. Families, friends, and neighbors gather to celebrate each night from December 16 through December 24.

Children and adults carry candles and walk behind figures of Mary and Joseph, recreating their journey to Bethlehem. They sing "Para pedir posada" as Mary and Joseph travel from place to place looking for shelter. The first part of this song is a plea, and the second part is an answer. Each time, the answer is that there is "no room" for the pilgrims.

PARA PEDIR POSADA

Looking for Shelter

MAP
UNITED STATES
MEXICO BELIZE
GUATEMALA

CD 21:22

Mexican Folk Song
English Version by MMH

Spanish: En__ nom - bre__ del cie - lo, Os__ pi -
Pronunciation: en nom bɾe ðel sye lo os pi
English: In__ the name_ of Heav - en, Hear_ my

do__ po - sa - da, Pues_ no pue - de an -
ðo po sa ða pwes_ no pwe ðe an
plea for shel - ter, My__ poor wife is wea -

dar, Mi__ es - po - sa a - ma - da.
ðaɾ mi es po sa a ma ða
ry, Do__ not send us a - way, We_ can - not go__ on.

CONCEPT
MELODY

SKILLS
SING

D *Response*   A7

A - quí no___ es me - són,   si - gan a - de-
a   ki   no   es   me   son   si   gan   a   ðe

No,___ I have___ no room for___ you here!   You must go   on,___ you

D   D7   G

lan - te,   yo___ no pue - do a - brir,
lan   te   yo   no   pwe   ðo   a   briɾ

can - not stay,   I have no room for   you___ to - day!

D   A7   D   A7   D

No___ sea al - gún tu -   nan -   te.
no   sea   al   gun   tu   nan   te

I   do not know who you are, you___ must___ go a -   way.

Perform "Para pedir posada" with half of the class singing
the first part and the other half singing the response.

After Mary and Joseph reach the place where they are welcomed, everyone sings "Entren, santos peregrinos" (Enter holy pilgrims). Then they celebrate by breaking the *piñata*, a brightly colored papier-mâche figure. The piñata is suspended in the air and is filled with treats. Children take turns breaking the piñata with a stick.

CD 21:26

Enter, Holy Pilgrims

Mexican Folk Song
English Version by MMH

Spanish: **En-tren san-tos pe - re-gri - nos, pe - re - gri - nos,__ Re - ci -**
Pronunciation: en tɾen san tos pe ɾe gɾi nos pe ɾe gɾi nos ɾe si
English: **En - ter in, all ho - ly pil-grims, ho - ly pil - grims.__ Wel-come**

ban es - te rin - cón, que aun-que es po - bre la mo - ra - da, la mo-
ßan es te ɾin koen keaun kes po ßɾe la mo ɾa ða la mo
to our hum-ble grove. There is lit - tle we can give you, we can

ra - da,__ Os la doy de co - ra - zón.
ɾa ða os la ðoi ðe ko ɾa son
give you,__ Still we wel - come you with love.

CONCEPT
RHYTHM

SKILLS
PLAY, SING

This song tells the story of a certain jolly gentleman who works all the year long to bring the gift of joy to children everywhere.

Listen for this rhythm pattern in "Once Upon a Christmastime."

Once Upon a Christmastime

CD 21:30

Words and Music by
Emily Crocker and John Higgins

1. Once up-on a Christ-mas-time, each year the sto-ry's told,

some-one brings hap-pi-ness to chil-dren young and old.

In his far - off fro-zen home, work - ing the

whole year through, build-ing toys for girls and boys, he

makes their dreams come true.

2. On and on the sto-ry goes as true as___ true can be,

each year it comes a-gain be-neath the Christ-mas tree.

With-in the heart of ev-'ry child, a tale that's as

old as time, for hap-py ev-er-af-ter-ing is once up-on a

Christ-mas, once up-on a Christ-mas, a sto-ry-book

Christ-mas, Christ-mas-time.___

CONCEPT
TONALITY
SKILLS
READ

To whom will you tell your Christmas wishes?

Jolly Old St. Nicholas

CD 22:1

American Carol

F   C   Dm   Am

Jol - ly old St. Nich - o - las   lean your ear this   way.

B♭   Am   Dm   G   C

Don't you tell a sin - gle soul   what I'm going to   say.

F   C   Dm   Am

Christ - mas Eve is com - ing soon,   now you dear old   man,

B♭   Am   Dm   Gm7   C   F

whis - per what you'll bring to me,   tell me if you   can.

The ideas expressed in this popular Christmas carol come from the Bible. Sing this song and let your joyful feelings show!

Use your arms to follow the melody. Move them down as the pitches go lower, and up as the pitches go higher.

Joy to the World

CD 22:5

Music by Lowell Mason
English Poem by Isaac Watts

Joy to the world! the Lord is come.

Let earth re - ceive her King.

Let ev - 'ry__ heart__ pre - pare__ Him__ room.__

And heav'n and na - ture__ sing, And__ heav'n and na - ture__ sing,

And__ heav'n__ and heav'n__ and na - ture sing.

The word *Kwanzaa* means "first fruits of the harvest." Kwanzaa is a time when many African American families celebrate their culture, history, and ancestors. This celebration lasts seven days, and uses words from Swahili, an African language.

On one of the days, Kwanzaa celebrates *Nia*, which means "purpose."

CD 22:8

Words and Music by Stan Spottswood

Ni - a stands for pur-pose of our peo-ple, of our

fam - i - lies, to make our com-mun - i - ties as great as

they can be. We can do this by tak - ing care _ of our

homes and com - mun - i - ties, and de - vel-op-ing the skills

and the know-ledge of our peo-ple. It's the peo-ple.

Sing Lo Lo Song from Senegal

The English words of this Senegalese song encourage you to dance and have a good time. Performing this song is a way to celebrate the Kwanzaa idea of Umoja, which means unity in Swahili.

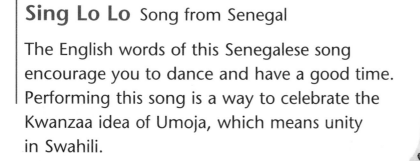

CONCEPT
FORM

SKILLS
SING

Martin Luther King, Jr. spoke out for peace and freedom. He believed in peaceful ways of protesting unfair treatment. Dr. King won awards for his actions and ideals about peace and equality for all people. On the third Monday of January we celebrate the life of this very important leader.

When we let freedom ring, when we let it ring from every village and every hamlet, from every state and every city, we will be able to speed up that day when [everyone] will be able to join hands and sing . . ., "Free at last! Free at last! Thank God Almighty, we are free at last!"

—*Martin Luther King, Jr.*

We Shall Overcome

CD 22:12

African American Spiritual
Adapted by Zilphia Horton, Frank Hamilton,
Guy Caravan and Pete Seeger

1. We shall o - ver - come. ___ We shall o - ver -
2. We are not a - fraid. ___ We are not a -
3. Black and white to - geth - er. Black and white to -
4. We are not a - lone. ___ We are not a -
5. Whole wide world a - round. ___ Whole wide world a -

come. ___ We shall o - ver - come some -
fraid. ___ We are not a - fraid to -
geth - er. Black and white to - geth - er
lone. ___ We are not a - lone to -
round. ___ Whole wide world a - round some -

day. ___
day. ___
now. ___ Oh, ___ deep in my heart, I do be -
day. ___
day. ___

lieve, Oh, oh, oh, we shall o - ver - come some - day.

CONCEPT
FORM
SKILLS
SING, IDENTIFY

Valentine's Day is a day to express your feelings for the ones you love. The message of this song is one of friendship. This song is written in a special style of music called the blues, but that doesn't mean it has to be sad!

I Will Be Your Friend

 CD 22:15

Words and Music by Guy Davis

Verse

1., 4. If you've got trou-bles and you need a help - ing hand,—
2. If you are hun - gry and you've got no place to stay,—
3. If you are lone - ly and you've got no-bod - y to love,—

If you've got trou-bles and you need a help - ing hand,—
If you are hun - gry and you've got no place to stay,—
If you are lone - ly and you've got no bod - y to love,—

If you've got trou-bles and you need a help - ing hand,—
If you are hun - gry and you've got no place to stay,—
If you are lone - ly and you've got no - bod - y to love,—

— Come to me, I— will be your friend.—

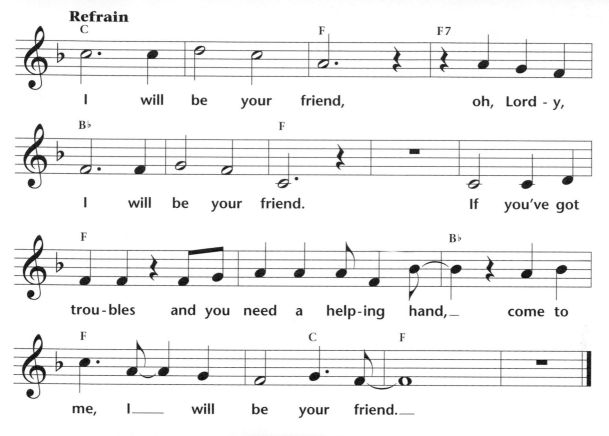

Refrain

I will be your friend, oh, Lord - y,

I will be your friend. If you've got

trou-bles and you need a help-ing hand,— come to

me, I will be your friend.—

Write one more verse to "I Will Be Your Friend."

 LISTENING CD 22:18

My Friend Mark Kibble and Joel Kibble

Friends are true to each other in good times and in bad.
Listen to this song about friendship, performed by Ray
Charles and the group Take 6. It tells about the meaning of
being a good friend.

Seasonal Songs

When spring arrives, the colors and sounds of the season begin to break through the cold of winter days and nights.

Sing this song about spring in Switzerland.

L'inverno è già passato

Winter Is Over

MAP

SWITZERLAND
ITALY
FRANCE
SPAIN

CD 22:19

Swiss Folk Song
English Words by Linda Worsley

Italian: L'in - ver - no_è già pas - sa - to, l'a - pri - le non cé più, è
Pronunciation: lin vɛr noe ja pas sa to la pri le non che pyu e
English: 1. The win - ter - time is gone now, and A - pril is no more. And
2. The moun - tain tops are bare, All the snow has gone a - way. Poor

rit - or - na - to_il mag - gio al can - to del cu - cù.
rit or na toil ma jo al kan to dɛl ku ku
May will bring the cuck - oo to sing out - side our door.
cuck - oo now is build - ing his nest through out the day.

Cu - cù, cu - cù, l'a - pri - le non cé più, è
ku ku ku ku la pri le non che pyu e
Cuck - oo, cuck - oo, Now A - pril is no more, and
Cuck - oo, cuck - oo, The snow has gone a - way. Poor

rit - or - na - to_il mag - gio al can - to del cu - cù.
rit or na toil ma jo al kan to dɛl ku ku
May will bring the cuck - oo to sing out - side our door.
cuck - oo now is build - ing his nest through out the day.

390

Spring from *The Four Seasons* by Antonio Vivaldi

"Spring" is the first of four concertos for violin from *The Four Seasons*. It has been a favorite ever since it was first performed.

 Use *Orchestral Instruments* **CD-ROM** to learn more about the violin.

Listening Map for Spring

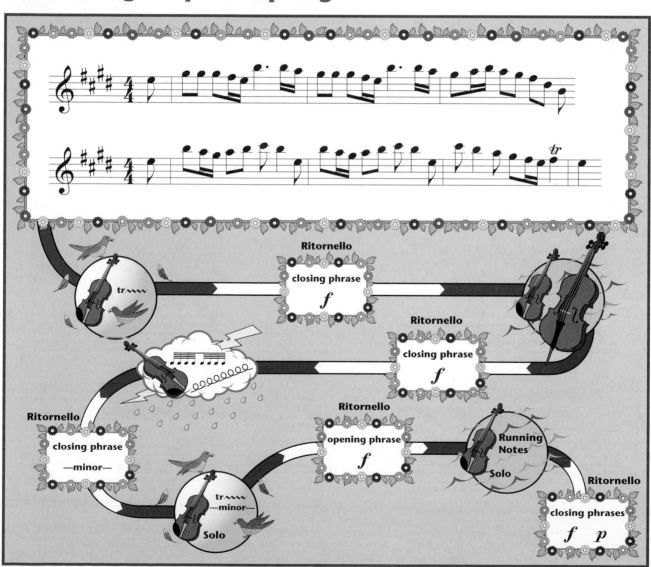

CONCEPT
RHYTHM
SKILLS
READ

The Laotian New Year is celebrated in April. It is a time of great festivity that lasts for days. On the first day of the new year, people go to the temple and pray for good health and prosperity for the coming year.

For the remaining days of the celebration, people put on a parade with songs and dance.

Dok Djampa

The White Jasmine Flower

MAP
MYANMAR
LAOS
THAILAND
KAMPUCHEA   VIETNAM

CD 22:24

Traditional Laotian
English Words by MMH

Laotian: ໂອ ດວງ ຈໍາ ປາ   ເວ ລາ ຊົມ ນ້ອງ
Pronunciation: o duang jʌm pʔa   ve la som nɔng
English: **Oh Dok Djam - pa___   our Jas-mine flow'r,**

Laotian: ນຶກ ເຫັນ ພັນ ຊ້ອງ   ມອງ ເຫັນ ຫົວ ໃຈ ເຮົາ ນຶກ ຂຶ້ນ
Pronunciation: nʊk hɛn pʌn sɔng   mɔng hɛn huə jai hau nʊkˀ kʊn
English: **the sight of you___   brings thoughts of home. Your beau-ty**

The *dok djampa,* a white jasmine flower, is the national flower of Laos. It can be found growing everywhere, from the countryside to the cities. It is often found growing near temples, where its lovely fragrance fills the air. The flower represents sincerity and the joy of life.

Sing this traditional Laotian song.

Use *World Instruments* **CD-ROM** to learn more about Southeast Asian instruments.

CONCEPT
METER
SKILLS
READ, SING

On Earth Day we are reminded to look at the world around us and to learn about what needs to be done to protect its beauty. This song reminds us of the Earth's beauty and how important it is to care for our surroundings.

We Are Here

CD 22:28

Words and Music by Sharon Burch

be,   to be.
And   we   are   here   to take
And   we   are   here   to

care of   our-selves,   to take   care of   one an-oth-er,   to take
love __   our-selves,   to   love __   one an-oth-er,   to

care of   our sur-round-ings.   Take care   to care.
love __   our sur-round-ings.   To love,   to love,   to

love.   *Navajo:* Na-has-dzáán   a-nii-la   ni-zhó-ní-go shaa hoł-ya
Pronunciation: na has dzan   a   ni   la   nɪ ʒɔ nɪ go sha hoł ya

zhó-ní-go   shaa   hoł-ya,   Hey,   hey-ey-o,
ʒɔ nɪ   go   sha   hoł   ya   hel   hel   i   yo

Hey-o, hey-o, hey-o.   Hey, hey-ey-o,   Hey-o, hey-o, hey-o.
hel yo hel yo hel yo   hel hel i yo   hel yo hel yo hel yo

Meet the Musician

The song "We Are Here" was written by **Sharon Burch**, a Navajo composer whose music is based on the songs that her grandfather, a Navajo medicine man, would sing during ceremonies. She has performed in many countries in the world, but always enjoys returning home to perform for her people.

Seasonal Songs

The ulili, or sandpiper, is a seabird. Ulili is also the Hawaiian name for a bamboo flute which sounds like the sound of the ulili's song—"to-li-li-li-li." The ulili announces the arrival of predators with its call. "´Ulili E" tells of the musical nature of the ulili bird. This Hawaiian folk song is often performed at Hawaiian Aloha Festivals that begin in August and end in October.

´Ulili E

The Sandpiper

CD 22:32

Traditional Hawaiian Folk Song
English Text by John Higgins

Hawaiian: Ho - ne a - na ko le - o e ´u - li - li e, I ka - hi
Pronunciation: ho ne a nʌ ko le o e ´u li li e i ka hi
English: Can you hear the sand - pi - per call a - cross the shore? O lit - tle

ma - nu no - ho ´a - e ka - i, Ki - a - ´i ma ka la - e a ´o ke-
ma nu no ho ´a e ka i ki a ´i ma ka la e a ´o ke
bird dart - ing through the foam - y sea. Yes, ev - er watch - ful is he up - on the

ka - ha, ´O - i a kai u - a la - na ma - li - e.
ka ha ´o i a kai u a la na ma li e
wa - ter, He makes his home where the sea is al - ways calm. __

´U - li - li e A - ha - ha - na ´u - li - li e he - he - ne ´u-
´u li li e a ha ha nʌ ´u li li e he hɛ ne ´u
Sand - pi - per calls

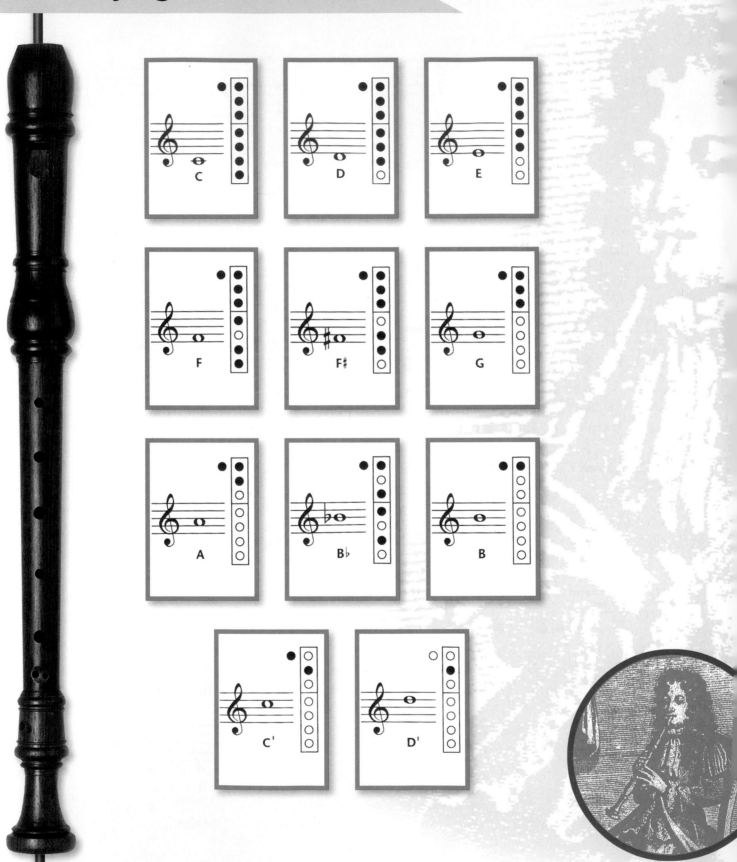

Glossary of Instruments

A

accordion a hand-held keyboard instrument that is played by pressing keys or buttons while air is forced through the instrument. It is often played while standing, and is held by straps over the shoulders, **CD 24:10**

B

bagpipe a member of the woodwind family that is played by blowing air through a tube into the bag and then pressing the bag so that the air is forced out through the pipes, **88 CD 24:11**

banjo a member of the string family that is played by plucking or strumming the strings, **31 CD 24:20**

bass drum a large member of the percussion family that gives a deep sound when hit, **CD 23:32**

bassoon a member of the woodwind family that is played by blowing into the reed while covering holes along the body with fingers, **CD 23:15**

C

cello the second-largest member of the string family in an orchestra, which is held between the knees and played by bowing or plucking the strings, **178 CD 23:6**

clarinet a member of the woodwind family that is played by blowing into the mouthpiece while covering holes along the body with fingers, **31 CD 23:12**

conga a percussion instrument used in Latin America that has a low-pitched sound when struck, **CD 24:30**

cymbal A dish-shaped percussion instrument that is often played by hitting one against another to make a clashing sound, **CD 23:37**

D

djembe a West African drum usually made from pottery or wood that is played with the hands, **CD 23:2**

double bass the largest instrument of the string family in an orchestra, which is held upright and played by bowing or plucking the strings, **CD 23:7**

flute a member of the woodwind family that is played by blowing across a hole at one end while covering holes along the body with fingers, **30 CD 23:10**

French horn a member of the brass family that is played by buzzing the lips into the mouthpiece while pressing keys with fingers, **CD 23:20**

güiro a Latin American percussion instrument that is made from a gourd and has a bumpy surface that is scraped with a stick to make a sound, **CD 24:33**

guitar a popular string instrument that is played by plucking or strumming the strings, **14 CD 24:13**

harp one of the oldest instruments in the string family, played by plucking or strumming the strings with fingers, **CD 23:8**

koto a long, flat, Japanese string instrument that is played by plucking its 13 strings, **CD 24:53**

mandolin a member of the string family that is similar to a guitar, but it has a different body shape and 8 metal strings, **CD 24:16**

maracas Latin American percussion instruments played in pairs by shaking when held at the handles, **CD 24:35**

oboe a double-reed woodwind instrument that is played by blowing into the reed while covering holes along the body with fingers, **CD 23:13**

piano a percussion instrument that is played by pressing the keys on the keyboard, **66 CD 23:41**

piccolo one of the smaller members of the woodwind family that is a small flute that plays high pitches, **CD 23:11**

saxophone a member of the woodwind family that is played by blowing into the mouthpiece while pushing the keys along the body with fingers, **CD 23:16**

shekere an African percussion instrument that is a hollow gourd covered with a net of beads or seeds and is played by shaking, **CD 24:8**

slit drum
a percussion instrument used in Africa, Asia, and the South Pacific that is formed by hollowing a tree trunk through a slit on one side and played by hitting with sticks, **CD 24:9**

snare drum
a member of the percussion family that is played by hitting the top of the drum with drumsticks to vibrate wires along the bottom, **31 CD 23:35**

spoons a common object used as a percussion instrument by holding two together and hitting them against the body. **14 CD 24:23**

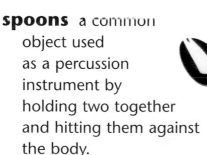

taiko drum
a barrel-shaped Japanese percussion instrument that is played with sticks, or *bachi*, **CD 24:51**

tambourine
a small, hand-held percussion instrument that has metal disks attached loosely around the rim and is played by shaking or hitting it with the hand, **31 CD 23:36**

timpani percussion instruments that are a set of large kettle-shaped drums, played with mallets and tuned to different pitches, **CD 23:26**

trombone a large, low-pitched member of the brass family, which is played by buzzing the lips into the mouthpiece while moving the slide in and out, **CD 23:21**

trumpet the smallest, highest-pitched member of the brass family, which is played by buzzing the lips into the mouthpiece while pressing keys with fingers, **CD 23:18**

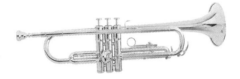

tuba the largest, lowest-pitched member of the brass family, which is played by buzzing the lips into the mouthpiece while pressing keys with fingers, **CD 23:22**

viola a member of the string family slightly larger than the violin, which is held under the chin and played by bowing or plucking the strings, **CD 23:5**

violin the smallest member of the string family in an orchestra, which is held under the chin and played by bowing or plucking the strings, **31 CD 23:4**

xylophone a percussion instrument that is played by hitting the wooden bars with small wooden hammers, or mallets, **CD 23:30**

Glossary of Terms

A

accent (>) a symbol that shows stress or emphasis on a note or chord, **282**

articulation how notes are played, **208**

augmentation changing a rhythm by making it last twice as long, **216**

B

bassoon a double-reed woodwind instrument that can play very low pitches, **116**

beat the pulse felt in most music, **6**

C

call and response a song form in which a phrase sung by a solo leader is followed by a phrase sung by a group, **70**

calypso a folk music style that was created in the Caribbean islands, **72**

candombe a style of music that was created in Uruguay, typically played for carnivals and festivals, **93**

canon a song form with two or more voices in which the melody is introduced and imitated one or more times, similar to a round, **16**

chord three or more pitches sounded together, **113**

contour the way a melody moves up and down, **12**

D

descant a second melody that is sung above the main melody of the song, **154**

downstage the space on the stage closest to the audience, **291**

duet music written for two performers, **9**

dynamics the loudness or softness of music, **106**

E

eighth notes (♪♪) musical notes that are half a quarter note, **15**

eighth rest a rest that equals one half a quarter rest.

F

flat (♭) a symbol in the key signature or in front of a note that means the pitch should be sung or played a half step lower, **110**

form the order of phrases or sections, or the plan, of a piece of music, **25**

fusion music musical traditions of more than one culture blended together, including compositions, styles, languages, and instruments, **208**

H

half note (♩) a symbol for a sound the length of two quarter notes, **15**

harmony two or more pitches sung or played at the same time, **111**

homophony blending two or more lines with the melody that have the same words and rhythm, to be in unison, **218**

J

jug a ceramic bottle that is used as an instrument in a jug band, played by buzzing the lips into the opening, **76**

jug band a band that uses simple items as instruments, such as jugs, washboards, and washtubs, **76**

K

key signature the sharps or flats at the beginning of each staff, **110**

L

ledger line a line added above or below the staff, **55**

legato in a smooth and flowing manner, **208**

letter names one way pitches on a staff can be identified, **71**

longways set a dance formation involving several pairs of dancers, the "head couple" at one end of the set and the "foot couple" at the other end, **51**

lullabies quiet songs sung to help babies go to sleep, **18**

M

major the sound of music that has *do* for its tonal center and uses the pitches of a major scale, **171**

major scale a specific set of eight pitches from *do* to *do'* **180, 186**

melody a series of pitches that moves upward, downward, or stays the same; a tune **11**

meter signature the symbol that tells how many beats are grouped in each measure and what kind of note equals one beat, **8**

minor the sound of music that has *la* for its tonal center and uses the pitches of a minor scale, **171**

minor scale a specific set of eight pitches from *la* to *la'* **186**

O

octave a leap of eight steps between two pitches, **129**

ornaments extra pitches or groups of pitches added to a melody to decorate it, **223**

ostinato a rhythmic or melodic pattern that repeats over and over, **37**

pentatonic scale a scale of five pitches, for example, *do re mi so la*, **21**

phrase a complete musical sentence or idea, **22**

polyphony the overlapping of two or more melodic lines, as in rounds, canons, and descants, **218**

presto very fast, **190**

program music story-telling or image-making music, **116**

---

quarter note (♩) the symbol for a note that equals two eighth notes, **15**

quarter rest (𝄽) a symbol for a silence the length of a quarter note, **15**

---

recorder a member of the woodwind family that has eight finger holes and is played by blowing into a mouthpiece, **97**

repeated notes notes sounding on the same pitch, **91**

rhythm the patterns of long and short sounds and silences in music, **15**

rondalla a group of plucked string instruments, **105**

root the pitch on which a chord is built, **143**

round a type of canon; a short song for three or more voices in which each voice begins at a different time, **16**

---

score written music that shows all the parts to be performed together, **28**

sections groups of related phrases that form a larger unit, **67**

skip one way a melody moves; to move higher or lower by jumping over a pitch, **91**

spiritual a song from the African American tradition that has religious meaning, **65**

staccato in a short and clipped manner, **208**

stage left the space to the left of the actor when facing the audience, **291**

stage right the space to the right of the actor when facing the audience, **291**

step one way a melody moves; to move higher or lower to the next pitch, **91**

syncopation a type of rhythm in which stressed sounds occur between beats instead of on beats, **139**

---

tempo the speed of the beat, **190**

tempo changes using different tempos to make music more expressive, **191**

theme the main musical idea of a piece, **236**

tie (⌣ or ⌢) a curved line that connects two notes of the same pitch and means that the sound should be held for the length of both notes, **139**

tonal center the home tone or the pitch around which a melody is centered, **21, 50**

tone color the special sound of each instrument or voice, **28**

triad a chord of three pitches, **148**

upstage the space on the stage farthest away from the audience, **291**

variation a changed version of a theme or melody, **236**

waltz a type of slow dance performed by a couple in which the music has three beats to a measure, **229**

washboard a grooved piece of metal set in a wooden frame that used to be used for scrubbing clothes and is played as an instrument in a jug band by scraping fingernails or fingers in thimbles across the metal piece to create a rhythm, **76**

washtub bass an instrument played in a jug band, built using a metal washtub, a broomstick or garden-tool handle, and some cotton or nylon line and whose pitch can be changed by moving the stick to tighten or loosen the single string, **76**

whole note a note that equals four quarter notes, **127**

woodwind a wind instrument that is or once was made of wood, **60**

N.Y.C., From MTI's Broadway Junior Broadway for Kids ANNIE Junior. Music by Charles Strouse. Lyrics by Martin Charnin. Music and Lyrics Copyright © 1977, 1978 by Edwin H. Morris & Co, a Division of MPL Communications, Inc. and Charles Strouse. All Rights Reserved. Used by Permission.

Octopus's Garden, Words and Music by Richard Starkey. Copyright © 1969 STARTLING MUSIC LTD. Copyright Renewed. All Rights Reserved.

Old Abram Brown, Words and Music by Benjamin Britten and Walter De La Mare. Copyright © by Boosey & Hawkes, Inc. International Copyright Secured. All Rights Reserved.

Once Upon a Christmas Time, Words and Music by Emily Crocker and John Higgins. Copyright © 1992 by Jenson Publications. International Copyright Secured. All Rights Reserved.

Over the Rainbow from THE WIZARD OF OZ. Lyric by E.Y. Harburg. Music by Harold Arlen. © 1938 (Renewed 1966) METRO-GOLDWYN-MAYER INC. © 1939 (Renewed 1967) EMI FEIST CATALOG INC. Rights throughout the World Controlled by EMI FEIST CATALOG INC. (Publishing) and WARNER BROS. PUBLICATIONS U.S. INC. (Print). All Rights Reserved. Used by Permission.

Peace Round, Old English Canon. Words by Jean Ritchie Adapted from Psalm 133: 1. Copyright © 1964 (Renewed 1992) by Jean Ritchie/Geordie Music Publishing Co. International Copyright Secured. All Rights Reserved. Used by Permission.

Peanut Vendor (El manisero), English Words by Marion Sunshine and L. Wolfe Gilbert Music and Spanish Words by Moises Simons. Copyright © 1928, 1929, 1931 by Edward B. Marks Music Company. Copyright Renewed. International Copyright Secured. All Rights Reserved. Used by Permission.

Please Mr. Postman, Words and Music by Robert Bateman, Georgia Dobbins, William Garrett, Freddie Gorman and Brian Holland. © 1961 (Renewed 1989) JOBETE MUSIC CO., INC. All Rights Controlled and Administered by EMI APRIL MUSIC INC. and EMI BLACKWOOD MUSIC INC. on behalf of JOBETE MUSIC CO., INC. and STONE AGATE MUSIC (A Division of JOBETE MUSIC CO., INC.). International Copyright Secured. All Rights Reserved. Used by Permission.

Roll On, Columbia, Words by Woody Guthrie. Music based on "Goodnight, Irene" by Huddie Ledbetter and John Lomax. TRO - © Copyright 1936 (Renewed), 1957 (Renewed) and 1963 (Renewed) Ludlow Music, Inc., New York, NY. International Copyright Secured. All Rights Reserved Including Public Performance For Profit. Used by Permission.

Sing Alleluia, Allelu, Words and Music by Mary Goetze. Copyright © 1984 by Boosey & Hawkes, Inc. International Copyright Secured. All Rights Reserved.

Sky Dances, Words by Jimmie Durham. Music by Roy Brown. Copyright © by Jimmie Durham and Roy Brown. International Copyright Secured. All Rights Reserved.

Something For Me, Something For You, Words and Music by J.D. Steele, Larry Long, Brian C. Herron and Nate Underwood. Copyright © 2003 by Southern Poverty Law Center. International Copyright Secured. All Rights Reserved.

Somos el barco (We Are The Boat), Words and Music by Lorre Wyatt. Copyright © 1985 by Lorre Wyatt/Roots & Branches Music. International Copyright Secured. All Rights Reserved.

Song of Thanksgiving, Words and Music by Robert de Frece from SINGING ROUND THE YEAR. Copyright © 2001 by Belwin. Copyright Secured. All Rights Reserved.

Step into the Spotlight, Words and Music by Emily Crocker, John Higgins and John Jacobson. Copyright © 2004 by HAL LEONARD CORPORATION. International Copyright Secured. All Rights Reserved.

Swing, The, Words by Robert Louis Stevenson. Music by John Chorbajian. Copyright © 1966 (Renewed 1994) by Canyon Press, Inc. International Copyright Secured. All Rights Reserved.

This Land Is Your Land, Words and Music by Woody Guthrie. TRO - © Copyright 1956 (Renewed), 1958 (Renewed), 1970 (Renewed) and 1972 (Renewed) Ludlow Music, Inc., New York, NY. International Copyright Secured. All Rights Reserved Including Public Performance For Profit. Used by Permission.

Tomorrow, From MTI's Broadway Junior Broadway for Kids ANNIE Junior. Music by Charles Strouse. Lyrics by Martin Charnin. Music and Lyrics Copyright © 1977, 1978 by Edwin H. Morris & Co, a Division of MPL Communications, Inc. and Charles Strouse. All Rights Reserved. Used by Permission.

Twist And Shout, Words and Music by Bert Russell and Phil Medley. Copyright © 1964 Sony/ATV Songs LLC and Sloopy II Music. Copyright Renewed. All Rights on behalf of Sony/ATV Songs LLC Administered by Sony/ATV Music Publishing, 8 Music Square West, Nashville, TN 37203. International Copyright Secured. All Rights Reserved.

Walking in the Air from THE SNOWMAN, by Howard David Blake. Copyright © EMI MUSIC PUBLISHING LTD. All Rights for the U.S. and Canada Controlled and Administered by EMI APRIL MUSIC INC. All Rights Reserved. International Copyright Secured, Used by Permission.

We Are Here, Words and Music by Sharon Burch. Copyright © 1999 by Canyon Records. International Copyright Secured. All Rights Reserved.

We Got the Beat, Words and Music by Charlotte Caffey. Copyright © 1981 by BMG Songs, Inc. International Copyright Secured. All Rights Reserved.

We Remember, Words and Music by Mac Huff and John Jacobson. Arranged by Mac Huff. Copyright © 2002 by HAL LEONARD CORPORATION. International Copyright Secured. All Rights Reserved.

We Shall Overcome, Musical and Lyrical Adaptation by Zilphia Horton, Frank Hamilton, Guy Carawan and Pete Seeger. Inspired by African American Gospel Singing, members of the Food and Tobacco Workers Union, Charleston, SC, and the southern Civil Rights Movement. TRO - © Copyright 1960 (Renewed) and 1963 (Renewed) Ludlow Music, Inc., New York, NY. International Copyright Secured. All Rights Reserved Including Public Performance For Profit. Used by Permission. Royalties derived from this composition are being contributed to the We Shall Overcome Fund and The Freedom Movement under the Trusteeship of the writers.

What Can One Little Person Do? Words and Music by Sally Rogers. Copyright © 2003 by Southern Poverty Law Center. International Copyright Secured. All Rights Reserved.

The Woodpecker, by Elizabeth Madox Roberts, from *Under the Tree*, copyright © 1922 by B.W. Huebsch, Inc., copyright © 1950 by Ivor S. Roberts. Reprinted by permission of The Viking Press, Inc. Reprinted in *Time for Poetry*, compiled by May Hill Arbuthnot, copyright © 1951, by Scott, Foresman and Company. All Rights Reserved.

You're Never Fully Dressed Without a Smile, From MTI's Broadway Junior Broadway for Kids ANNIE Junior. Music by Charles Strouse. Lyrics by Martin Charnin. Music and Lyrics Copyright © 1977, 1978 by Edwin H. Morris & Co, a Division of MPL Communications, Inc. and Charles Strouse. All Rights Reserved. Used by Permission.

Dream Dust by Langston Hughes, from *THE DREAM KEEPER and Other Poems*, by Langston Hughes. Published by Alfred A. Knopf. Copyright © 1994 by The Estate of Langston Hughes. All Rights Reserved. Used by Permission.

The Inward Morning by Henry David Thoreau, from *A Week on the Corcord and Merrimack Rivers*. Reprinted in *Walden and Other Writings of Henry David Thoreau*. Edited by Brooks Atkinson. The Modern Library, Copyright © 1937, 1950, 1963, by Random House, Inc. All Rights Reserved.

My Sister by Margaret Mahy, from *Nonstop Nonsense*. Reprinted in *Lots of Limericks*. Selected by Myra Cohn Livingston with permission of Margaret K. McElderry Books, an imprint of The Macmillan Publishing company. Copyright © 1991. All Rights Reserved.

One Song, America, Before I Go by Walt Whitman, from *Leaves of Grass and Other Writings*. Edited by Michael Moon. W.W. Norton & Company, Inc. Copyright © 1973, 2002. All Rights Reserved.

Rain Haiku by Mary Anne Mohanraj. Copyright © 1998. Used by Permission. Reprinted in *Piping Down the Valleys Wild*. Edited by Nancy Larrick. Published by Delacorte Press, Copyright © 1968, 1985. All Rights Reserved.

The Snail's Dream by Oliver Herford. Reprinted in *The Random House of Book of Poetry For Children*. Selected and introduced by Jack Prelutsky. Copyright © 1983 by Random House, Inc. All Rights Reserved.

Two Limericks, anonymous, reprinted in *Lots of Limericks*, Copyright © 1999. Selected by Myra Cohn Livingston with permission of Margaret K. McElderry Books, an imprint of The Macmillan Publishing Company. All Rights Reserved.

Trains at Night by Frances M. Frost, from *The Arbuthnot Anthology of Children's Literature*. Copyright © 1961 by Scott, Foresman and Company. All Rights Reserved.

Whispers by Myra Cohn Livingston, from *Whispers and Other Poems*. Copyright © 1958. Reprinted by permission of Harcourt, Brace & World, Inc. Reprinted in *Piping Down the Valleys Wild*. Edited by Nancy Larrick. Published by Delacorte Press. Copyright © 1968, 1985. All Rights Reserved.

Woodpecker, The by Elizabeth Madox Roberts, from *Under the Tree*. Copyright © 1922 by B.W. Huebsch, Inc. Copyright © 1950 by Ivor S. Roberts. Reprinted by permission of The Viking Press, Inc. Reprinted in *Time for Poetry*, compiled by May Hill Arbuthnot. Copyright © 1951, by Scott, Foresman, and Company. All Rights Reserved.

CREDITS

Illustration Credits: Paul Bachem: 104, 105, 128. Timothy Banks: iv, Spotlight on Concepts (2). Richard Bernal: 46-47. Shennen Bersani: 336. Ka Botzis: 103. Gina Capaldi: 10-11, 358-359. Antonio Castro: vi, Spotlight on Performance (2), 247, 305, 338. Bradley Clark: 168, 169, 178-179, 180-181. Renee Daily: 48-49. Bob Doucet: 312. Louise Ellis: 126-127, 380. Leslie Evans: 226-227. Peter Fasolino: 308-309. Tina Fong: v, Spotlight on Music Reading (2). Jo Gershman: 074-075. Renee Graef: 123. Shelly Hehenberger: vii, Spotlight on Celebrations (2). Jui Ishida: 337. John Kanzler: 30-31, 344. Diana Kizlauskas: 327, 328-329. Nora Koerber: 88-89. Erin Eitter Kono: 368, 385. Fran Lee: 232, 320. Margaret Lindmark: 340. Deborah Maze: 328. Yoshi Miyake: 345, 347. Suzanne Mogensen: 26-27. Cheryl Kirk Noll: 134-135, 136-137. David Opie: 98-99. Donna Perrone: 152-153, 378. Gary Phillips: 192-193. Stacey Schuett: 206-207. Charlie Shaw: 142-143. Janet K. Skiles: 122, 123. Adam Turner: 188-189. Sally Jo Vitsky: 330-331, 332-333. Siri Weber Feeney: 106, 108, 322-323, 324-325. Elizabeth Wolf: 92, 342.

Photography Credits: all photographs copyright of Macmillan/McGraw-Hill (MMH) except as noted below.

Allan Landau for MMH: cover, A-B, C-D, E-F, G-H, i, 42-43, 51, 58, 69, 70, 71, 82-83, 84, 85, 116, 118, 122-123, 129, 149, 179, 189, 202, 202-203, 237, 403, 404. Shane Morgan for MMH: 9, 33, 95, 96, 148, 151, 167, 171. Jim Powell for MMH: 40, 116.

A: t.r. Corbis; t.c.l. PhotoDisc, Inc. B: t.r. PhotoDisc, Inc. C-D: bkgd. PhotoDisc, Inc. G: c.r., b.r. PhotoDisc, Inc.; c.l. Corbis. G-H: bkgd. PhotoDisc, Inc. H: c.r. PhotoDisc, Inc. 2-3: c. Bob Daemmrich/ PhotoEdit, Inc. 4: c.l. Bob Daemmrich/PhotoEdit, Inc. 4-5: t. Hulton Archive|Getty Images; b. PhotoDisc, Inc. 5: A. Ramey/PhotoEdit, Inc.; r. PhotoDisc, Inc. 6-7: bkgd. Ariel Skelley/Corbis; bkgd. Corel. 8: b.l. National Gallery, London, UK/ Bridgeman Art Library/ Estate of Pablo Picasso/Artists Rights Society ARS, NY; t.r. Corbis. 9: t.r. Carol Friedman. 10-11: t. Corel; 12-13: Corel; 12-13: bkgd: Maury Christian/Corbis. 13: b.r. Angel Millan/AP/Wide World Photo. 13: b.r. Courtesy of Fox Products Corporation, South Whitley, IN, US. 14: b.r. PhotoDisc, Inc 14-15: bkgd. Artville, LLC. 15: b.r. Arville. 16-17: Corel. 17: c.r. Florida Today/Slawsongs; t. Lebrecht Music Collection. 18: bkgd. Bob Rowan/Corbis. 19: b.c.r. Geoffrey Clements/Corbis; bkgd. Bob Rowan/Corbis; c.r. Bob Rowan/Corbis. 20-21: bkgd. The Newark Museum/Art Resource, NY. 22-23: bkgd. PhotoDisc, Inc. 23: b.l. PhotoDisc, Inc.; b.r. Corbis; c.r. Gai Terrell/Redferns Music Picture Library. 24: b.c. , b.l. Roger De La Harpe/Corbis; b.r. David Turnley/Corbis; t.r. Patrick Robert/Corbis. 24-25: bkgd. Dover Publications, Inc. 26-27: t. MetaCreations/Kai Power Photos. 28-29: bkgd. Corel; t. MetaCreations/Kai Power Photos. 35: t.r. Keith Mallet. 36-37: bkgd. PhotoDisc, Inc. 38: Courtesy of Fox Products Corporation, South Whitley, IN, US. 44: b.l. Comstock. 45: t. PhotoDisc, Inc. 48: b.r. Marg Hewson. 50-51: bkgd. Bettmann/Corbis. 52-53: bkgd. Corbis. 54-55: bkgd. Nathan Benn/Corbis; t. Corel. 55: PhotoDisc, Inc. 56: b.r. Shelley Gazin/Corbis; t.r. Lucasfilms. 56-57: bkgd. Lucasfilms; t. Corel. 58: b.l., t.l. Corbis; b.r., c.r. PhotoDisc, Inc. 59: r. Corel. 60: b.l. Kelly Mooney Photography/Corbis; b.r. Roger De La Harpe/Corbis; c.r. Archivo Iconografico, S.A./Corbis; t.r. PhotoDisc, Inc. 60-61: b. Corel. 61: b.l. Liu Liqun/Corbis; b.r. Viviane Moos/Corbis; c.r. Archivo Iconografico, S.A/Corbis; t.r. PhotoDisc, Inc. 62-63: bkgd. Bettmann/Corbis. 64: Playback Magazine; c.r. PhotoDisc, Inc. 64-65: bkgd. Corbis. 65: c., t. Corel. 66-67: bkgd. Wolfgang Kaehler/Corbis. 67: t.r. Corbis. 68: b.r. Christie's Images/Bridgeman Art Library. 68-69: bkgd. Richard T. Nowitz; t. Corel. 70-71: bkgd. Larry Luxner. 72-73: b.r. Digital Vision/Punchstock. 74-75: bkgd. PhotoDisc, Inc. 75: bkgd. Ernesto Gomez. 76: b.r. Cathy Crawford/Corbis; c. PhotoDisc, Inc.; c.r., t.r. Ernesto Gomez. 77: b.c.l., b.l. Mark Wagoner Productions; b.r., c.l. Ernesto Gomez. 80: t.r. PhotoDisc, Inc.. 86-87: bkgd. Michael Maslan/Corbis. 90-91: bkgd. M. Timothy O'Keefe/Bruce Coleman, Inc. 91: c.r. Travelsite/Colasanti/The Picture Desk. 93: c.r. AFP/Getty Images; t.l. AP/Wide World Photos. 96: Almari/Art Resource, NY. 100: l. Corbis. 101: r. Dave G. Houser/ Corbis; t. Julian Coche Mendoza/Arte Maya Tz'utuhil. 104: b. Hinata Haga/HAGA/The Image Works; c. Joe Carini/Pacific Stock. 105: b.l. Paul A. Souders/Corbis; t.c.l. Hinata Haga/HAGA/The Image Works. 106-107: bkgd. PhotoDisc, Inc. 108: b.r. Horace Bristol/Corbis; c. Corbis. 108-109: bkgd. Australian Picture Library/Corbis. 109: t.r. Horace Bristol/Corbis. 110-111: bkgd. Hugh Beebower/ Corbis. 112-113: bkgd. Richard T. Nowitz/Corbis. 113: b.r. Judith Yellin-Ginat. 114: t.r Billy Rose Theatre Collection, The New York Public Library for the Performing Arts, Astor, Lenox and Tilden Foundations.114-115: b.c.l., b.l., t.r. PhotoDisc, Inc.; t. MetaCreations/Kai Power Photos. 116: Lebrecht Music Collection; b.c.r. Corbis; b.l., b.r., c.r., t.c.r. PhotoDisc, Inc. 117: Courtesy of Fox Products Corporation, South Whitley, IN, US; 1., 2., 3., 4., b.c.r., b.l., b.r., c.r. PhotoDisc,Inc. 120: b.r. PhotoDisc, Inc. 121: b.r., c.r. PhotoDisc, Inc.; t. The U.S. Army Field Band; b.l. PhotoDisc, Inc.; t.r. James Shaffer/PhotoEdit, Inc. 124: Comstock; t. Corbis; t.r. Carol Rosegg Photography. 128: r. PhotoDisc, Inc.; t.r. PhotoDisc, Inc. 128-129: b. Corbis. 130-131: bkgd. PhotoDisc, Inc. 131: t.r. Philadelphia Museum of Art/Corbis. 132-133: bkgd. Charles & Josette Lenars/Corbis. 134: c.r. Wolfgang Kaehler/Wolfgang Kaehler Photography. 137: b.r. Georgette Douwma/ ImageState-Pictor/PictureQuest. 138-139: b. Robert Frerck/Odyssey Productions; bkgd. North Wind Picture Archives. 140: b.l. Tiziana and Gianni Baldizzone/Corbis; b.r. Hideo Haga/HAGA/The Image Works, Inc. 140-141: bkgd. Alamy Images, Ltd.; t. Robert Frerck/Odyssey Productions. 141: b.c. Tiziana and Gianni Baldizzone/Corbis. 141: b.l. Philadelphia Museum of Art/Corbis; b.r. North Wind Picture Archives. 143: AP/Wide World Photos. 144: b.r. Lebrecht Music Collection; b.l. Dave Bartruff/ Corbis; c.r. Volker Dornberger/DPA /Landov. 144-145: bkgd. Corel. 146: Corel. 146-147: bkgd. Arville, LLC. 148-149: bkgd. PhotoDisc, Inc. 150-151: bkgd. Jeremy Woodhouse/Getty Images. 153: Pool/Kirsty Wigglesworth/Reuters Newmedia, Inc./Corbis. 154-155: bkgd. Tria Giovan/Corbis. 156-157: bkgd. Corbis. 157: 1., 2. PhotoDisc, Inc.; 3., 4. Corbis. 162: b. David Hiser/Stone/Getty Images; bkgd. Corbis. 162-163: c. AP/Wide World Photos; t. Keren Su/Corbis. 164: t.r. MetaCreation/Kai Power Photos. 164-165: bkgd. Corbis. 166-167: bkgd. EPA/Jon Hrusa/AP/Wide World Photos. 167: Corbis. 168-169: t. Bo Zaunders/Corbis. 169: t.r. Hamburg Kunsthalle, Hamburg, Germany/Bridgeman Art Library. 170-171: bkgd. Corbis. 172: b. Corbis. 173: c. Bojan Brecelj/Corbis; t.r. PhotoDisc, Inc. 174: t. Giraudon/ Bridgeman Art Library. 174-175: bkgd. Corbis. 175: b.r. Stapleton Collection, UK/Bridgeman Art Library; t.r. Giraudon/Bridgeman Art Library. 176: r. North Wind Picture Archives; t.r. Corbis. 176-177: bkgd. Corbis. 177: b.r. Rheinisches Bildarchiv/Wallraf-Richartz Museum Koln- Fondation Corboud; t.l. Lebrecht Music Collection. 178-179: t. MetaCreations/Kai Power Photos. 180-181: t. MetaCreations/Kai Power Photos. 181: c.r. Erich Hartmann/Magnum Photos. 182-183: bkgd. Corbis. 183: t.r. Corbis. 184: b.c., b.l. , b.r., Mary Gotze; bkgd. Neil Beer/Corbis. 186-187: bkgd. Alain Le Garsmeur/Stone/Getty Images. 190-191: bkgd. Robbie Jack/Corbis. 191: t.r. Robbie Jack/Corbis. 195: t. Kelly-Mooney Photography/Corbis; t. PhotoDisc, Inc. 196-197: bkgd. Michael Short. 197: c.r. J. Michael Short/Vargas; t.r. Multi-Ethnic Cultural and Arts Association. 198: PhotoDisc, Inc. 199: t. MetaCreations/Kai Power Photos. 200: c.r. PhotoDisc, Inc. 204: l. Bettmann/Corbis; t.r. Reuters NewMedia Inc./Corbis. 205: t.r. Corbis. 206-209: t. Corel. 208: b.r., c.r. Image Club Graphics. 208-209: bkgd. Corel. 209: b. David Atlas/Retna, Ltd.; r. Jack Vartoogian. 210-211: bkgd. ML Sinibaldi/Corbis. 210-213: t. Corbis. 211: t.r. Dave Bartruff /Corbis. 212: b.l. Dave G. Houser/ Corbis; b.r. Image Farm, Inc.; b.r. PhotoDisc, Inc.; t.r. Morton Beebe/Corbis. 212-213: bkgd. Larry Lee Photography/Corbis. 213: t.r. Annebicque Bernard/ Corbis Sygma. 214-215: bkgd. Terje Rakke/Image Bank/Getty Images. 216: b.l. Elins Eagles-Smith Gallery; b.r., t.r. PhotoDisc, Inc. 216-217: bkgd. Corbis. 217: b.r., t.r. PhotoDisc, Inc. 218-219: b., t. Marilyn Root/Index Stock Imagery. 222: bkgd. Reunion des Musees Nationaux/Art Resource, NY; c.l. Victoria & Albert Museum, London/Art Resource, NY. 223: bkgd. Reunion des Musees Nationaux/Art Resource, NY; t.r. Attar Maher/Corbis Sygma. 224: b.l. Colin Paterson/PhotoDisc, Inc./Getty Images; b.r. Ludovic Maisant/Corbis. 224: Image Club. 224-225: bkgd. Historical Picture Archive/Corbis. 225: b.l. Christopher Cormack/Corbis; b.r. Owen Franken/Corbis; t.r. Annebicque Bernard /Corbis/Sygma. 225: b.r. G. Salter/Lebrecht Music Collection. 226-229: t. Corel. 228: t. Jim Cooper AP Photo. 228: b.r., l. Jack Vartoogian. 230-231: bkgd. Jeremy Horner/Corbis. 230-233: t. Corel. 232: t.r. Herman Leonard/Redferns Music Picture Library. 233: t.r. Corbis. 233: Stockbyte PunchStock. 234-235: bkgd. MetaCreations/Kai Power Photos. 236-237: bkgd. Christine Osborne/ Worldwide Picture Library/Alamy. 238: b.r. PhotoDisc, Inc. 242: t.l. Corbis. 261: b.l. Corel. 262: t.l. PhotoDisc, Inc. 263: b.l. PhotoDisc, Inc. 264: b.l. PhotoDisc, Inc. 267: b.l. PhotoDisc, Inc. 268: b.l. Corel. 271: b. PhotoDisc, Inc. 276: b. Corbis. 290: b. MTI; c.l. Corel; c.l. PhotoDisc, Inc. 291: r. Artville. 292: b.r. PhotoDisc, Inc. 295: c.r. PhotoDisc, Inc. 297: b.r. PhotoDisc, Inc. 298: c.r. MTI. 300: b.r. ImageClub. 303: b.r. MTI. 305: b.r. PhotoDisc, Inc.; c. MTI. 306: t.r. Bettmann/Corbis. 307: t.r. PhotoDisc, Inc. 309: t.r. PhotoDisc, Inc. 310: b.l. Bettmann/Corbis; t.r. Lambert/Archive Photo/Hulton Archive|Getty Images. 311: t.r. PhotoDisc, Inc. 313: t.r. PhotoDisc, Inc. 314: t.l. Bettmann/Corbis. 315: t.r. PhotoDisc, Inc. 316: b.l., b.r., l., t.l. Photodisc, Inc.; c.l. Stockbyte; t.r. Rubberball. 317: t.r. PhotoDisc, Inc. 319: b.r. Everett Collection. 325: b. Bob Daemmrich/Stock, Boston, Inc./PictureQuest. 325: c. Craig Aurness/Corbin. 326: r. PhotoDisc, Inc.; t.l. PhotoDisc, Inc./Getty Images. 327: t.r. PhotoDisc, Inc. 328: b. Mark Lewis/Picturesque/PictureQuest. 329: t.r. PhotoDisc, Inc. 331: t.r. PhotoDisc, Inc. 333: t.r. PhotoDisc, Inc. 335: t.l. Ariel Skelley/Corbis; t.r. PhotoDisc, Inc. 337: t.r. PhotoDisc, Inc. 339: t.r. PhotoDisc, Inc. 341: t.r. PhotoDisc, Inc. 343: b. Terry Cryer/Corbis; t.r. Corel. 345: t.r. PhotoDisc, Inc. 347: t.r. PhotoDisc, Inc. 349: t.r. PhotoDisc, Inc. 351: b. Galen Rowell/Corbis; t.r. PhotoDisc, Inc. 356: t.r. The Granger Collection. 362: t.l., t.r. PhotoDisc, Inc. 363: b.r. PhotoDisc, Inc. 364: b.l., b.r., t.l. PhotoDisc, Inc. 365: b. Art Resource, Inc. 367: c.l. Corbis; c.r. Philippe Giraud/Corbis. 370: t.l., t.r. PhotoDisc, Inc. 372: bkgd., t.r. PhotoDisc, Inc. 373: b.r. Artville, LLC. 374: t.l. Image Club Graphics. 375: b. Art Resource, NY. 375: t.r. MetaCreations/Kai Power Photos. 375: b. The Art Archive/Fondation Maeght St. Paul de Vence/Dagli Orti. (c)Artists Rights Society (ARS), New York/ADAGP, Paris. 376: b. Keith Dannemiller/ Corbis; b.l. PhotoDisc, Inc.; c.l. AP/Wide World Photos; c.r. Corbis. 382: b.l. Getty Images; b.r., t.r. PhotoDisc, Inc. 383: t.r. Corel. 384: t.l. Comstock; t.r. PhotoDisc, Inc.; t.l. Richard Lord/PhotoEdit, Inc. 385: t.r. Corbis. 386: b.l. Hulton Archive|Getty Images; b.r. Flip Schulke/Corbis; c.r. Ernst Haas/Hulton Archive|Getty Images. 389: b. PhotoDisc, Inc.; b.l. Corbis. 392: c. Garden City Telegram/AP Photo; c.l. Nevada Wier/Corbis; c.r. Alison Wright/Corbis. 393: b.r. Corbis. 395: b.r. John Running/Canyon Records. 399: c.l. PhotoDisc, Inc./Getty Images; c.r., t.l. PhotoDisc, Inc. 400: b., b.r., t.l. PhotoDisc, Inc.; b.r. Jules Frazier/PhotoDisc, Inc./Getty Images. 401: b.r., c.r. PhotoDisc, Inc. 403: t.l., t.r. PhotoDisc, Inc. 404: b.r., c.l. PhotoDisc, Inc.

All attempts have been made to provide complete and correct credits by the time of publication.

Classified Index

YOUR BROADWAY MUSICAL

INDEX OF POETRY

Alphabetical Index

Global Voices

Interviews

INDEX OF SONGS AND SPEECH PIECES

Pronunciation Key

Simplified International Phonetic Alphabet
VOWELS

ɑ	f<u>a</u>ther	o	<u>o</u>bey	æ	c<u>a</u>t	ɔ	p<u>aw</u>
ə	ch<u>a</u>otic	u	m<u>oo</u>n	ɛ	p<u>e</u>t	ʊ	p<u>u</u>t
i	b<u>ee</u>	ʌ	<u>u</u>p	ɩ	<u>i</u>t	ə	<u>a</u>go

SPECIAL SOUNDS

β	say *b* without touching lips together; *Spanish* nue<u>v</u>e, ha<u>b</u>a
ç	<u>h</u>ue; *German* i<u>ch</u>
ð	<u>th</u>e; *Spanish* to<u>d</u>o
ɳ	sound <u>n</u> as individual syllable
ö	form [o] with lips and say [e]; *French* a<u>dieu</u>, *German* sch<u>ö</u>n
œ	form [ɔ] with lips and say [ɛ] *French* c<u>oeu</u>r, *German* pl<u>ö</u>tzlich
ɾ	flipped r; bu<u>tt</u>er
r̄	rolled r; *Spanish* pe<u>rr</u>o
ɬ	click tongue on the ridge behind teeth; *Zulu* <u>ng</u>cwele
ü	form [u] with lips and say [i]; *French* t<u>u</u>, *German* gr<u>ü</u>n
ᴜ̈	form [ʊ] with lips and say [ɩ]
x	blow strong current of air with back of tongue up; *German* Ba<u>ch</u>, *Hebrew* <u>H</u>anukkah, *Spanish* ba<u>j</u>o
ʒ	plea<u>s</u>ure
´	glottal stop, as in the exclamation "uh, oh!" [´ʌ ´o]
~	nasalized vowel, such as *French* b<u>on</u> [bõ]
˥	end consonants *k*, *p*, and *t* without puff of air, such as s<u>k</u>y (no puff of air after *k*), as opposed to *kite* (puff of air after *k*)

OTHER CONSONANTS PRONOUNCED SIMILAR TO ENGLISH

ch	<u>ch</u>eese	ny	o<u>ni</u>on; *Spanish* ni<u>ñ</u>o
g	<u>g</u>o	sh	<u>sh</u>ine
ng	si<u>ng</u>	ts	boa<u>ts</u>

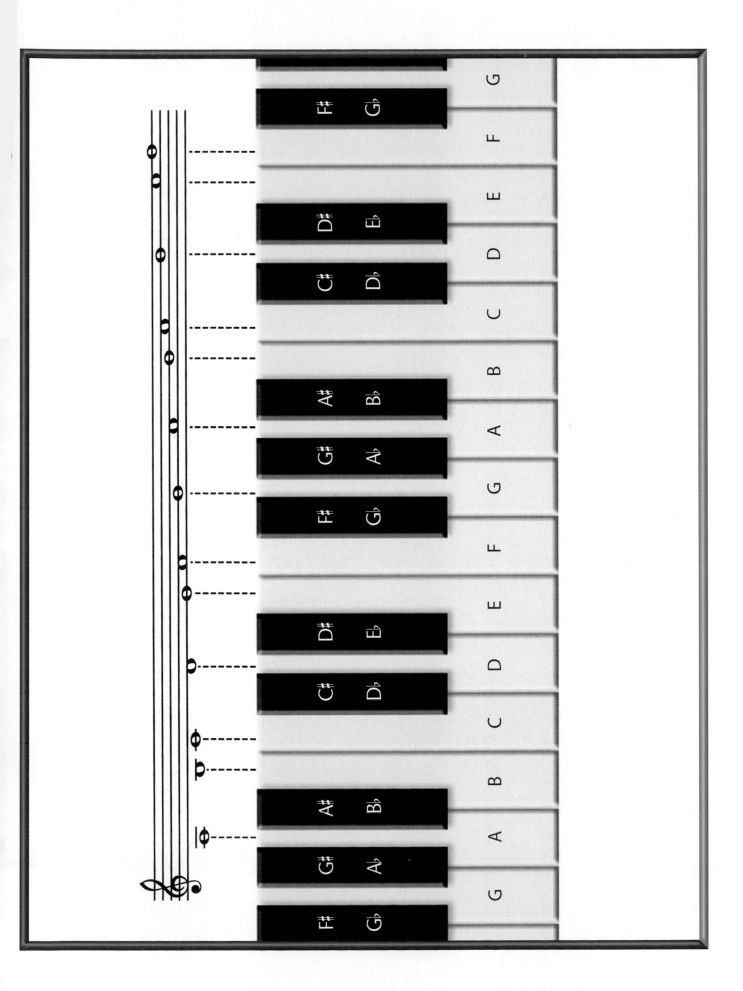

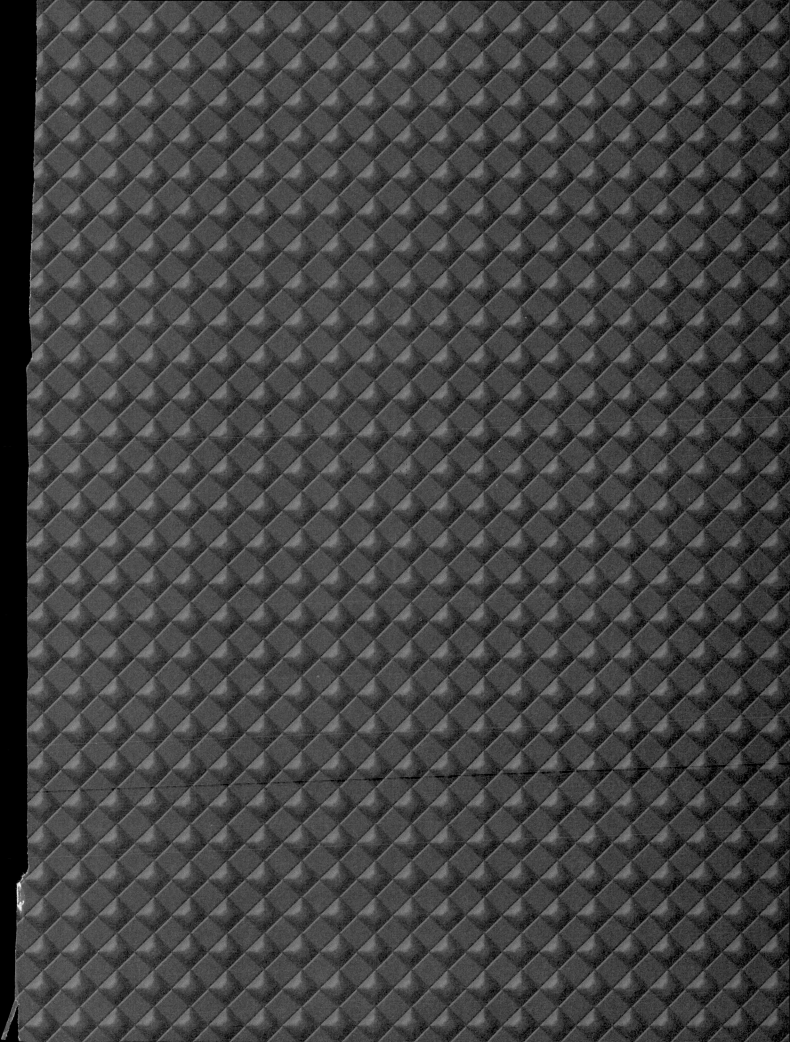